great little things to make on a small lathe

great little things to make on a small lathe

David Regester

B T Batsford Ltd, London

To Christine

First published 1995

© David Regester, 1995

Typeset and designed by David Seabourne
and printed in Great Britain by Butler and Tanner,
Frome, Somerset

Published by
B.T. Batsford Ltd
4 Fitzhardinge Street
London W1H 0AH

A catalogue record for this book is available from the
British Library

ISBN 0 7134 7613 3

Contents

PART ONE:
Tools, Equipment and Materials

PART TWO:
Small Items for the Home

Spindle Projects

Hollowing Projects

PART THREE:
Furnishings for Dolls' Houses

Acknowledgements

I would like to thank those firms who supplied me with tools and machinery to use in the preparation of this book, namely: Axminster Power Tool Centre, Craft Supplies Ltd, Tyme Machines, Reg Sherwin, Crown Tools Ltd and Bonnie Klein.

Preface

A wide array of useful and attractive miniatures and little items can be made on a small lathe. The main purpose of this book is to provide ideas for turning a range of objects and to detail the sequences you need to follow in order to make them. I have presented the projects in order of increasing difficulty in the hope that the turning skills needed for each one will be acquired gradually. Working through the projects in this book should enable you to put your own design ideas into practice.

The emphasis throughout, however, is more on how and what to make rather than tool technique which has already been covered in my other books. The projects are grouped in sections and, as they are mainly intended to provide inspiration for those who have some basic skills (perhaps as a result of having prac-tised the techniques in my first book, *Woodturning: Step-by-Step*) but who lack a huge budget and sufficient space for a full-size lathe and large chunks of wood, I have not named the tools, techniques or chucks needed for each specific item. Whatever your level of experience, I hope that this book will provide a source of ideas which will help you to experiment with and enjoy turning wood.

Part One: Tools, Equipment and Materials

If you are starting from scratch, you will not only need to buy a lathe, but also some turning tools, a bench grinder (with a stone dresser) for sharpening them, some wood and probably a workbench on which to place the lathe (as the cheaper models are not normally equipped with their own stands).

At the time of going to press, there is a good selection of small lathes on the market in the UK for less than £300 new; a bench grinder will set you back about £70 and you can probably expect to spend from around £40 on a basic tool kit. The cost of the wood will vary infinitely depending on its type and quality as well as on the size and shape of the objects you decide to make. Of course, prices will change but this should give an indication of the relative cost of getting started.

1 Clarke CWL6B

The Lathe

The table below shows some of the lathes that are currently available for less than £300. They are all small in so far as they are made to fit on workbenches although they do vary considerably in terms of length, power and speed. Unlike large pedestal or floor-standing lathes, they are not capable of turning bigger pieces of work and cannot be used for very extended periods of time.

How to decide which lathe to buy

When buying a lathe, no matter what size, it pays to take your time and seek the advice of as many other people as you can, including specialist shops, woodworking teachers and members of turning clubs. Firstly you have to decide what type of turning you

Model	Maximum length between centres mm (in)		Diameter over bed mm (in)		Motor hp	Number of speeds	Range of speeds rpm
APTC KWL37	940	(37)	305	(12)	0.5	5	480–2980
Carba-Tec	300	(12)	150	(6)	0.16	4	700–2800
Clarke CWL12C	940	(37)	305	(12)	0.5	5	475–3260
Clarke CWL6B	500	(19¾)	242	(9½)	0.5	4	850–2510
Draper WTL 12	940	(37)	305	(12)	0.5	5	480–3010
Klein Design Inc.	305	(12)	127	(5)	0.16	6	500–5200
Nu-Tool NWL37	940	(37)	305	(12)	0.5	5	483–3012
Poolewood 12-37	940	(37)	305	(12)	0.5	5	575–3580
Record CLO 24 x 12	600	(24)	305	(12)	0.33	3	450–2000
Record DML 24X	600	(24)	225	(9)	0.33	3	450–2000
Record RPML 300	305	(12)	225	(9)	0.33	3	450–2000
Rema DNSA-100	1000	(39⅜)	300	(11¾)	0.5	3	400–2000
Sealey SM42	940	(37)	305	(12)	0.75	5	480–2980
Tyme Little Gem	230	(9)	104	(4)	0.25	variable	0–5000

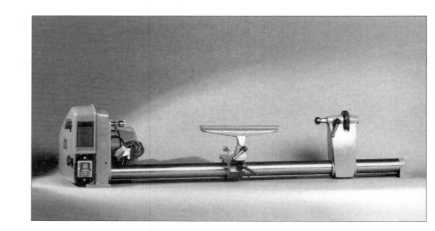

2 *APTC KWL37*

3 *Author using Carba-Tec lathe*

are most interested in. For instance, if you just want to turn lace bobbins you will only need a small lathe. If you are not sure what you want to turn, you would be better advised to buy a small, well-engineered lathe rather than a larger, cheap one. The latter type will have a bigger capacity but may be made to a less exacting standard, resulting in poor performance. This could cause you to make mistakes which, if you are not sure of your ability, you blame yourself for without realizing that, say, the lathe itself does not run true. It is also worth noting that a small but well-made lathe should hold its value for resale.

4 Clarke CWL12C

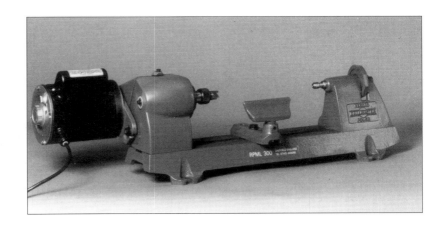

5 Record RPML 300

6 Carba-Tec

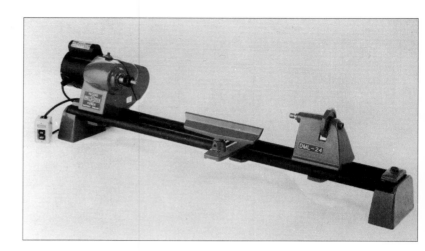

7 Record DML 24X

When you have decided what sort of lathe you actually want, consider your budget, bearing in mind the other equipment you will need (as specified on page 8) and the possible extras described below.

Hidden extras

When buying a small lathe check what is supplied with it. You may need to buy some pieces of equipment separately. Listed below are the most essential:

Faceplate
Most small lathes do not come with a faceplate.

Driving centre
A four-prong centre is usually supplied but you may need one of a different size or prefer a two-prong centre.

Dead centre
A lathe will often come with only one of these and you will almost certainly find that a revolving centre is better.

Switch
Take a good look at the switch. Woodturners tend to turn the lathe on and off much more often than many manufacturers seem

to think, so see if you can operate it easily. Sometimes the switch is in an awkward place such as on top of the motor, whereas it is actually easier to use one which is on the front. A rocker switch in a heavy dust proof cover will be difficult to press, while a rocker switch without any cover at all may jam open with shavings. A mushroom-type off-switch, which just needs to be pushed to turn it off, is best. Most manufacturers of inexpensive lathes save on the switch. They are not intended for use in the professional workplace so do not have a 'No Volt Release' facility, which means that if there is a power cut or if you turn off the lathe at the plug, it will start up again when power returns with potentially dangerous results. For maximum safety and ease of use it is definitely worth spending approximately another £40 on a decent 'No Volt Release' switch.

8 Klein Design Inc. with Bonnie Klein's pieces

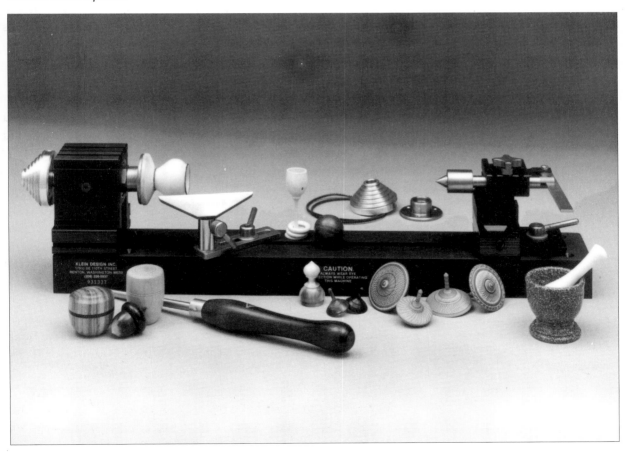

Motor

Some lathes are not provided with a motor and, whereas this will certainly save on electricity, you will not get much turning done if you do not remedy the situation! Ask for advice from your lathe supplier as to the most suitable motor. Do not choose an enormously strong one for a small lathe because the belt that takes the power from the motor to the pulley will be too weak to convey the extra power.

The motors provided for most lathes, if they are single-phase, vibrate at 100 cycles if the supply is 50 cycles and 120 if it is 60 cycles – this is a natural function of single-phase motors. If the motor is mounted on a platform which is attached to the headstock, look at the mounting to check if it is possible to loosen it so that vibrations are not transmitted through the headstock on to the work. If there is a facility for adjusting the position of the motor by means of a bolt, you may be able to loosen the bolt. Alternatively, it may be possible to reduce the vibration by putting tap washers between the motor and the motor platform. If you do this, avoid tightening up the screws too much as tap washers are made of very hard rubber and, when compressed, can transmit vibrations. Modifications like this can improve the performance of your lathe but you should always be careful that you do not make the equipment dangerous or invalidate the guarantee. When in doubt, consult the manufacturer.

Rest

Most small lathes come with only one short rest but you will probably need a longer one if you intend to turn longer pieces of work. Do look closely at the rest when buying the lathe because the shape may not suit you (it is largely a matter of what you are used to, but at least it should be designed to support the tool close to the work) and also check that it has been well made. Rests of different shapes are available from equipment suppliers.

Rest adjustment

Most importantly, you should be able to raise and lower the rest from below the centre of the work to a little above it and to move the rest support arm easily. On some lathes (such as the Record DML 24X) these adjustments must be done with Allen keys or spanners, which is tedious. If this is the case, you may want to superglue an Allen key into the socket or ask your supplier for an alternative, such as Bristol locking handles. It is better if the adjustment bolt is either made of brass or has a brass core. If it is made of a metal as hard as that of the rest support column, in the course of time, this will tend to dent the column and eventually make adjustment very difficult.

Tailstock

This should slide up and down the bed easily but should stay in place once tightened up. It should be hollow bored for easy removal of centres and the adjustment of the quill is best done by means of a knurled wheel with a handle. Again, you should be able to lock the quill in place.

Attachment for an electric drill

This is the cheapest way of starting to turn, but there are some major disadvantages. The drill should not be used for longer than 20 minutes at a time and, as the bearings on DIY drills are mounted in plastic allowing for some side play, you can never work accurately with them. It is necessary to have a professional drill with the bearings mounted in metal to use these attachments satisfactorily, but one of these will cost over £100.

Chucks

There are some very good chucks available for use on full-size lathes such as those made by Craft Supplies, Axminster Power Tools, Multistar, Record and Nova (addresses can be found on pages 93–94) and, for an even wider choice, you can always follow up adverts in the woodworking press. All chucks have their advantages and disadvantages and have been reviewed in the past by the magazines; you make your choice on the usual basis of what you need, what you can afford and blind prejudice.

There are chucks designed specially for use on the small lathe, for example the Craft Supplies Mini-Grip 1000 (photo 9) and the Multistar Micro (photo 10). A Jacob's chuck (or similar type), obtainable from the lathe manufacturers specifically to fit the lathe, works very well and is usually intended to be used in the tailstock or headstock for drilling. It is most commonly attached to a morse taper arbor that fits in either or both positions, but if it is you cannot use it in the headstock to hold work unless you support the work at the other end with the tailstock. Otherwise, any sideways thrust from a tool will tend to cause the morse taper to work loose in the spindle. This is rather unfortunate because a

9 Craft Supplies Mini-Grip 1000 on Carba-Tec

Jacob's chuck is very useful for a small lathe, particularly for dolls' house pieces. It is possible to make a Jacob's chuck usable in this situation by taking a chuck from a drill and finding a bolt with the same thread that is long enough to pass through the spindle. In the case of the Little Gem, the bolt was too fat to go through, so I turned it down to the correct diameter. I then drilled and tapped the end so that I could insert a screw to prevent the bolt from coming out of the spindle. You can obtain such a shaft as an accessory for the Klein Design Inc. lathe and it will also fit the Little Gem.

10 Multistar Micro

Tools

The projects featured on pages 29–53 can all be made using a set of spindle tools (as described in detail in *Woodturning: Step-by-Step* and *Turning Boxes and Spindles: Step-by-Step*), which can be seen in photo 11. Figs. 1–3 show clearly the shape of the bevels on my own tools, but this is a matter of personal preference.

My recommended basic spindle kit comprises a 19mm (³⁄₄in) roughing gouge, a beading and parting tool, a 10mm (³⁄₈in) oval section skew chisel (the top three tools in photo 11) and a 10mm (³⁄₈in) spindle gouge. Instead of a purpose-made spindle gouge, you can use a carving gouge if you can get a second-hand one cheap (bottom in photo 11) and for parting off you can add either a fluted parting tool as seen in photo 11 or a thin parting tool as in Fig. 4. The fluted parting tool is used with the flute downwards and the Crown Tools parting tool is used in the orientation shown in the illustration. Both are used in the up and over style shown in Fig. 8 on page 24.

If you want to turn a stool top or Lazy Kate base or even a bowl, you will need to get some bowl-turning tools. These are different from spindle tools which are not safe for use on bowls. Roughing gouges have prominent corners that can catch inside bowls. Spindle gouges are thinner than bowl gouges and can bend or break on faceplate work. It is highly dangerous to use a skew chisel when the grain is running at right angles to the axis

Fig. 1 Roughing gouge

Fig. 2 Spindle gouge

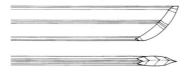

Fig. 3 Skew chisel
Oval section Curved edge

Fig. 4 Crown Tools thin parting tool

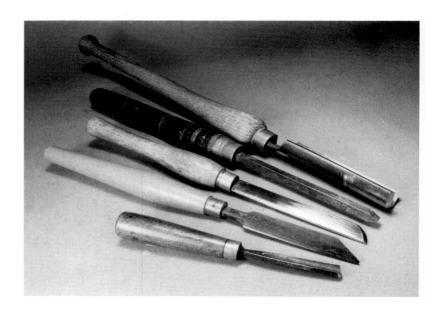

11 Set of spindle turning tools

because it will invariably catch. The basic bowl-turning kit I recommend is a 10mm (³⁄₈in) bowl gouge and a 19mm (³⁄₄in) round-nosed scraper.

If you intend to concentrate exclusively on small work, tool manufacturers now make sets of mini and micro tools which are cheaper than buying the full sized equivalents. In photo 12 you can see a set of micro tools from Craft Supplies and photo 13 shows the mini and micro sets produced by Crown Tools. The micro set in photo 13 features twice as many tools as at first

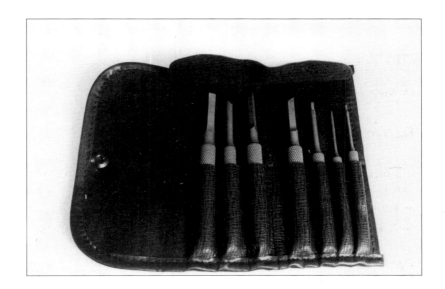

12 Craft Supplies micro tools

13 Crown Tools mini turning set and micro turning set

appears because the shafts are held in the handles by Allen screws and are sharpened at both ends. It is even possible to get a set of miniature hollow form tools developed by Chris Stott from his full size version for turning hollow form vessels.

Sharpening

It is absolutely vital to keep your tools sharp so that they cut cleanly. Blunt tools cause accidents because you need to press harder to get them to cut.

For sharpening, use a bench grinder with two aluminium oxide wheels which are best for high speed steel. I use a 60 grit wheel for radically altering a tool's shape and a 100 grit wheel to form a good edge. Keep the wheels in good shape by dressing them regularly. The tool can be used straight from the grinder. You need a concave bevel to enable you to rub the bevel to support the edge when turning. To achieve this hold the tool so that the edge is at right angles to the wheel. Obviously, when the tool has a curved edge it must be moved in an arc to cover the whole edge. Look for the grooves left by the wheel on the bevel and you should soon see whether they are running at right angles to the edge.

Start sharpening at the shoulder of the tool and work towards the edge so that you do not spend too much time with the wheel pressing on the thinnest part of the tool which could lose its temper if it is allowed to overheat. There is no need to press the tool hard on the wheel; the grits cut quickly enough without you having to do this and you only blunt the grits and overheat the tool if you do press. Should you find that the tool starts to turn blue, you must not plunge it in water. High speed steel is tempered by being air cooled and water cooling does not do it any good. Blueing means that the metal has been hardened without being tempered. You may not notice the difference in use but if you do, you will just have to grind away the blueness gently.

It is very difficult for the novice to sharpen tools correctly and I strongly recommend that a grinding jig is used to get the angles right. These range in price and efficacy from the O'Donnell jig and sharpening charts at the top of the range, to the do-it-yourself plans in Keith Rowley's book, but they are all easier to use than the rests provided by most grinder manufacturers.

Abrasives

There are many different types of abrasive on the market. Garnet paper is the cheapest worth using but you do need to buy the open coat version, which clogs less easily, and also the lightest grade of paper so that you can bend it around tight curves. This paper has a tendency to lose its grits when damp or where folded.

The best abrasive is aluminium oxide on a cloth backing and resin bonded; because the grits are harder, they do not loosen and the bonding prevents clogging. It is more expensive than garnet paper but lasts much longer. It is water and oil proof so you can use it soaked in water or finishing oil, which lubricates the grits. This means that not only does the abrasive remain effective longer, with the material removed being carried away in the liquid rather than clogging the spaces between the grits, but also the presence of liquid on the surface of the abrasive makes the grain stand up so that a finish is achieved much more quickly. There is also little possibility of heating the wood with friction. Instead of dust you produce gunge which is much less dangerous for the lungs, but you do tend to splash the walls and, if you stand in the wrong place, your face.

Abrasives come in degrees of coarseness, the lowest number being the coarsest. I recommend 80, 120, 180 and 240. They can be bought by the roll or in sheets.

When sanding work on the lathe, you must remove the rest and hold the paper in such a way that it is carried away from your fingers; in other words, under the lathe with your palm facing up. If you fold the paper in three, you will be protected against the heat but be prepared to cut the abrasive into smaller pieces for finely detailed work.

The best sanding technique is to use the coarsest grit to get rid of tool marks or rough grain, only moving on to a finer grade when all such marks have been removed. It is no use thinking that as you progress through the grades the original defects will disappear because they will not. The main function of the finer grades is to remove the marks left by the previous grade. Always keep the paper moving to prevent grooves forming and do not press too hard as you will only blunt the grits. It is best to use the coarsest grits at a slow speed, gradually increasing the spindle speed as you progress through the grades.

Timber

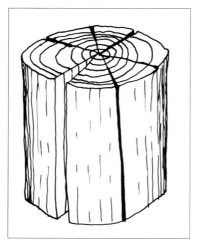

Fig. 5 Short log with radial shakes

Where a certain type of wood is highly suitable for one of the projects, I have mentioned it in the text, but on the whole, you can use most of the hardwoods available from timber suppliers. To practise techniques, the wood does not have to be seasoned, but if you want the finished piece to remain as you made it, it is important that the moisture content is stable for the environment in which it will be kept. Timber is often sold as air dried even when it is not and disappointment will result unless you take care that the wood you are using is actually dry. In other words, do not buy a piece of wood and expect to be able to use it immediately; you may have to season it yourself (see below).

One source of cheap, ecologically sound wood is a tree that has outlived its useful life in a garden, park or orchard. You can often obtain the wood from such trees by informing friends or neighbours that you have a use for it or by contacting tree surgeons or park departments. You will need to own (or hire) and know how to use a chainsaw to take advantage of this source.

Seasoning wood

To season wood, keep it out of the rain and sun and allow air to circulate around it. Air drying takes approximately 12 months per 25mm (1in) of thickness but to minimise splitting, which takes the form of radial shakes in short logs (Fig. 5), you must prevent the wood from drying out too quickly from the ends by covering them with old oil-based paint or end grain sealer (emulsified paraffin wax). To release the tension that builds up when the ends dry, split the log (Fig. 6) or cut it lengthways with a chainsaw. If the wood is to be used for turning spindles, it will dry more quickly and with less splitting if you first cut it into square-sectioned pieces of the dimensions you will need.

Grain

For spindles and projects such as boxes and pepper mills, the grain should run parallel to the bed of the lathe, partly because long, thin wooden objects will be strengthened if this is the case but also because it is very much easier to turn them with the grain

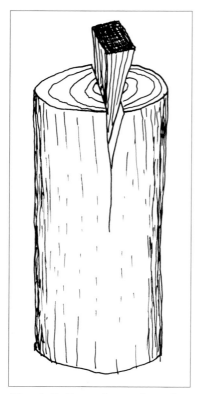

Fig. 6 Splitting log with wedge

Fig. 7 The parts of a tree

❶ Best used for practising techniques as the heart running through it usually causes splitting unless it has been seasoned long and slow

❷ Often has the most dramatic grain, which may look attractive, but can make turning difficult (particularly spindles). This type of wood often splits when drying

❸ Lumps that grow on the outside of a tree, often in response to insect or fungal attack, but in some cases a tree will be composed entirely of burr wood. The grain has many small knots and the most beautiful figure of all. Best used for bowls as it can be very difficult to turn as spindles

❹ Where the grain runs straightest. Ideal for turning spindles

❺ Often seen as a lump either at the bottom of the trunk or just below the start of the crown. It can be found on some ornamental and fruit trees where, in the nursery, the variety with the desirable feature was grafted to a rootstock. The figure in the graft is often very attractive

❻ Roots have a completely different grain from the rest of the tree because they perform a separate function. Not often used (except in the case of walnut where they are used for gunstocks) because, not unnaturally, they often contain stones which tend to damage saws

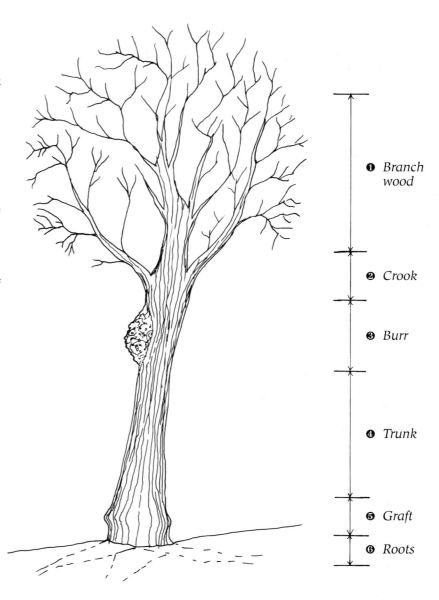

❶ *Branch wood*

❷ *Crook*

❸ *Burr*

❹ *Trunk*

❺ *Graft*

❻ *Roots*

in this alignment. For objects such as honey dippers, which have thin handles, do not select a very curly grained piece of timber or you will not have one annular ring running the whole length of the handle; in other words, there will be short grain which will weaken the handle. It is also important to avoid highly figured wood for runs of spindles (e.g. stool legs) because each piece will be noticeably different and will also be difficult to turn quickly.

Tips on Technique

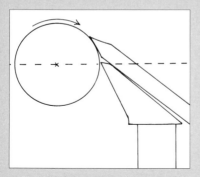

Fig. 8 Correct use of beading and parting tool

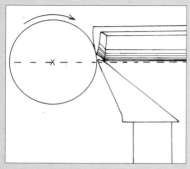

Fig. 9 Incorrect use of roughing gouge

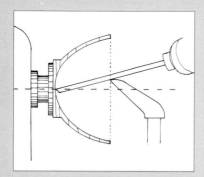

Fig. 10 Using a scraper – rest above centre, tool pointing down

This book is not intended to be a manual of techniques, but it is always worth mentioning the absolute rules for safety reasons. Some general guidelines are also listed here to remind you when to use certain tools and how to do so correctly. These are basic principles and you should not be afraid to experiment with new techniques and alternative ways of using tools.

Absolute rules

❑ Always rotate the timber by hand before starting the lathe to ensure that it does not snag against the rest.

❑ Always check the speed of the lathe before starting it and, if you are in any doubt about the speed, start slowly and then work faster.

❑ Always put the tool on the rest before allowing the edge to touch the work.

❑ Never wear loose clothing or allow hair or jewellery to dangle on to the lathe.

❑ Always wear eye protection and a dust mask.

❑ Never leave a chuck key in the chuck.

General rules

There are some exceptions to the following but you should read through them all carefully.

❑ Gouges and chisels should be used pointing upwards with the rest below centre height. (Figs. 8 and 9 show the tools being used correctly and incorrectly respectively).

❑ Scrapers should be used pointing downwards with the rest above centre height (Fig. 10).

❑ When turning bowls and flatware, the rest should be positioned so that the tool in its correct cutting position will be able to cut the centre of the work.

❑ Gouges are used with the flute pointing in the direction of the cut.

❑ Gouges and skews are generally used so that the angle between the work and the tool is greater on the side of the work which is about to be cut than on the side which has been cut.

- Avoid standing to the side of work held at only one end (such as on a faceplate) as this is the direction it will go if it becomes detached.

- Tools should be kept sharp at all times and the bevels should be concave. If you have trouble recognising which part of the tool you have sharpened, use a felt-tip pen to colour the bevel.

- The bevel should rub lightly on the work while the tool is being used. If you are unsure as to the angle at which the tool should be held, rub the bevel on the work and gradually bring the edge into contact. When you first use a tool this exercise can be done before the lathe is started up, rotating the work by hand to ensure that the tool is at the correct angle. Even when you are more practised, you can still do this, with the lathe running.

- Chattering is a common problem and manifests itself as ripples on the work which cause the tool to make a rattling noise as it passes across them. This has several possible causes, the most typical being that the tool is blunt. It can also be caused by the tool being held so that the bevel is rubbing too hard against the work or so that it is at the incorrect angle i.e. not with the oblique angle in the direction of cut. It is a common fault to hold the tool too near the horizontal, in which case it is generally a good idea to try again with the handle lower than you had it when the chattering occurred. The rest may also require adjustment; try it higher, lower or closer to the work. You could also try a different speed or perhaps cut in the opposite direction.

- When rolling a bead with a skew chisel, use the point of the tool (Fig. 11a–d) rather than part of a long edge because it will be easier to control while making this complex cut.

- Always cut with the grain so that the fibres you are cutting are supported by the fibres underneath. On spindles this is downhill whereas when hollowing end grain it is from inside out and when hollowing bowls, with the grain running at right angles to the axis of the lathe, it is from outside in.

- For a cheap, non-toxic and easy-to-use finish, apply cooking oil or liquid paraffin when the work is still and buff when rotating, rubbing in a little wax. You can use Danish or tung oil for finishing articles that will not come into direct contact with food.

Fig. 11a–d Rounding a bead with the point of a skew

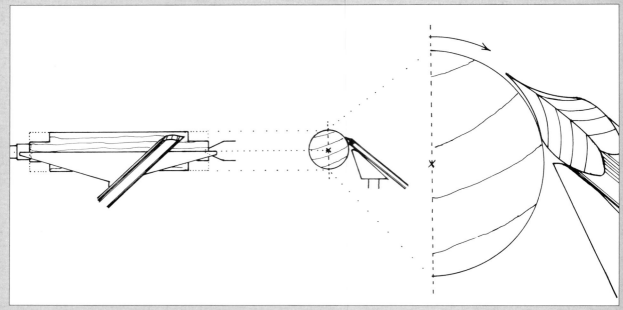

a Bevel rubs against work but the edge is not in contact and therefore will not cut

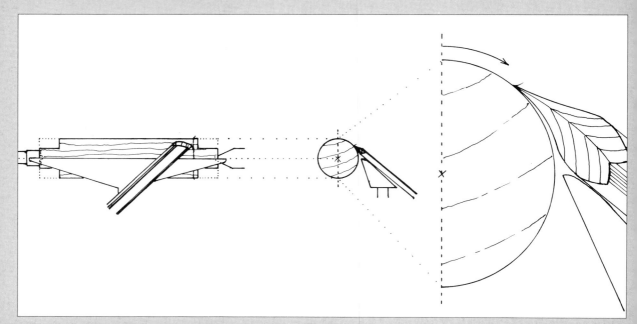

b Tool is twisted so that the point is in contact and will cut

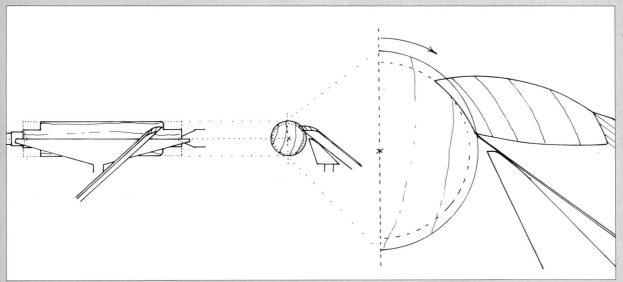

c *The tool rolls over and cuts the shoulder*

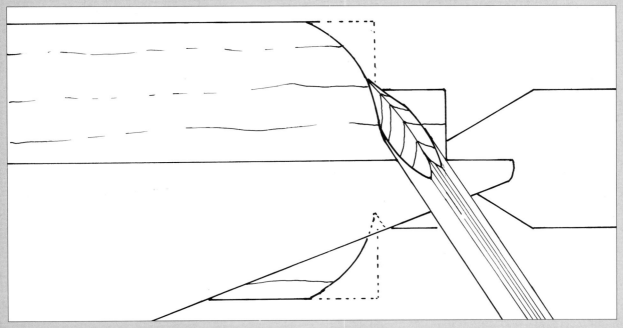

d *At the end of the cut the tool is on its narrow face and the angle at rest is 90° from where it began. The tool handle is raised, thereby lowering the tip as the cut progresses*

Part Two: Small Items for the Home

Spindle Projects

A whole variety of objects can be made on a small lathe between centres. Many of these can be put to good use around the house and, consequently, will be much appreciated when given away as presents or sold. Although they are not particularly difficult to make, they constitute very good exercises and will help you to master some of the most important turning skills.

Rolling Pin

TIMBER

50mm (2in) x 50mm x 230mm (9in) of odourless, close- and straight-grained timber such as ash, sycamore, London plane or any fruit-wood

LATHE SPEED

1330 – 2250 rpm

CHUCKING

Between centres

Turning

Shape the main contours of the rolling pin with a roughing gouge, forming a 12mm ($\frac{1}{2}$in) spigot at both ends using the beading and parting tool or parting tool. Put a pencil mark 40mm (1$\frac{1}{2}$in) from each end and form a bead and cove using a beading and parting tool, a gouge or the point of a skew. Plane the roller smooth using either the skew or the gouge. The handles must be 6mm ($\frac{1}{4}$in) smaller than the centre of the rolling pin. Ensure that the rolling portion is straight and smooth and of the same diameter at each end. Check this with a straightedge and callipers. Sand and finish the rolling pin and then part off.

Depending on the use to which you will put the rolling pin, both the handles and the body may be increased in length with a corresponding increase in diameter if required. Any increase will also depend on the length of the bed of the lathe.

14 Ash rolling pin

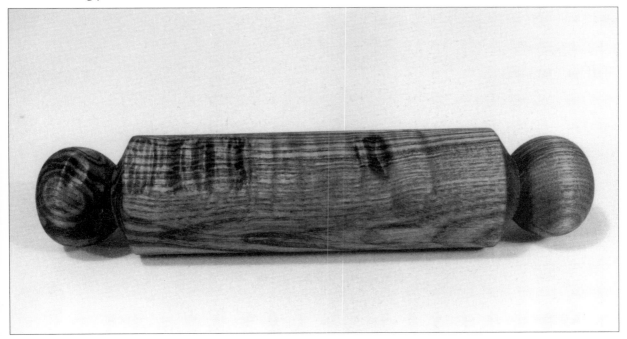

Steak Basher

TIMBER

65mm (2 ½in) x 65mm x 230mm (9in) of odourless, close- and straight-grained timber such as ash, sycamore, London plane or any fruit-wood

LATHE SPEED

1330 – 2250 rpm

CHUCKING

Between centres

Turning

Create the basic shape of the steak basher with a roughing gouge. Form a 12mm (½in) spigot at each end and make the head 90mm (3½in) long, shaping the remaining wood into the handle.

Plane the head section true and straight with a skew or gouge. Cut grooves in the head of the basher with the point of the skew, starting at the end away from the handle. Cut a thin vertical line and then enlarge each side of this as shown in Fig. 12a and b. If you find it hard to space the grooves evenly, mark them out with a pencil and ruler before starting the lathe. The dots should be visible as continuous lines but if they are faint you can always hold the pencil on them as the work rotates to make them clearer.

When you have made sufficient grooves, shape the junction of the head and handle. This should be fairly steep so that you can hold the handle close to the head, but the beauty of making such items yourself is that you can shape them to suit the size of your hand by frequently stopping the lathe and trying the fit. If you are making them for sale, you need to aim for a happy medium or make a range of sizes. It is best to make the end of the handle slightly flared to prevent the hand from sliding off. Sand and finish the steak basher and then part off.

15 Ash steak basher

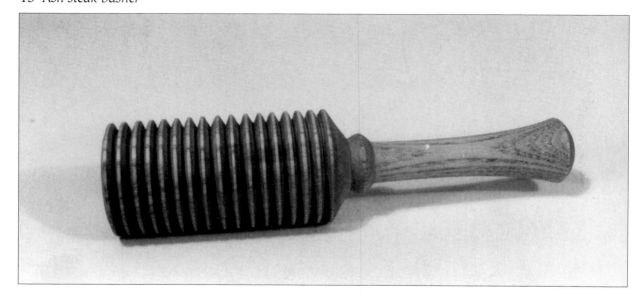

Fig. 12a–b Steak basher

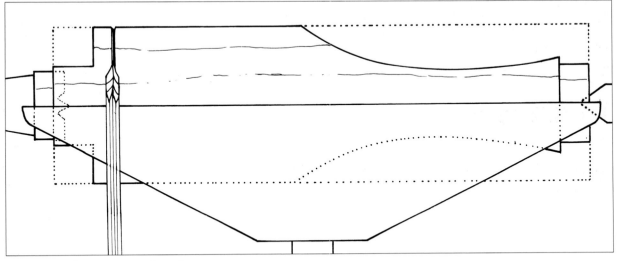

a *Starting the groove with a skew*

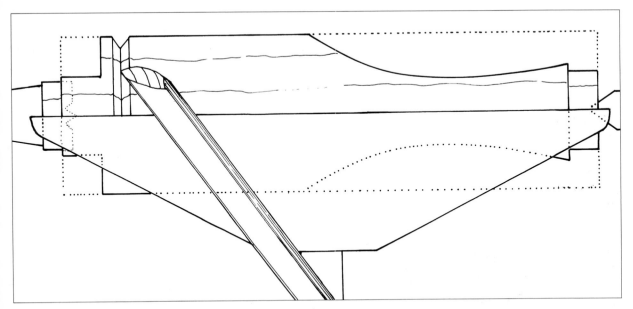

b *Cutting the right-hand side of the groove with a skew*

Honey Dipper

Turning

Rough out the basic shape of the honey dipper using a skew with a curved edge. Turn a spigot at either end and finish shaping with the point of the skew. The head of the honey dipper is grooved to maximise the surface area so that it can hold more honey (see page 30 for the method of turning grooves). Finally, sand, finish and part off.

16 Ash honey dipper

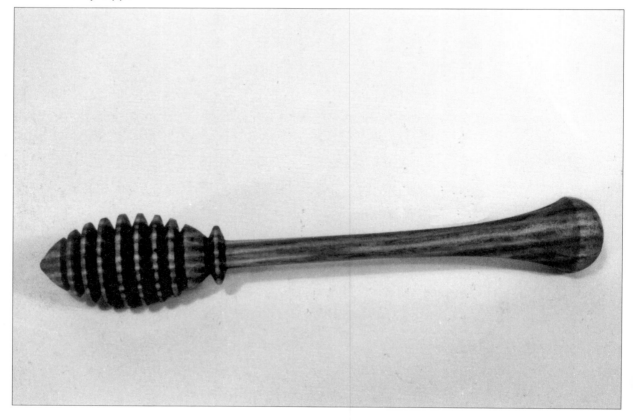

Stool Leg

Design

The best way of designing a stool leg is to take a piece of inexpensive wood (preferably softwood), put it between centres and experiment with it until you create a pleasing shape. I prefer long, flowing curves to a complicated series of beads and coves. It is easier to replicate the latter because there are more reference points for you to measure, but producing a long, flowing curve will show that you are an accomplished turner.

You will see that photo 18 features a stool leg with a ball foot which ensures good contact with the floor at whichever angle the leg is set in the stool seat. If you make a vertical stool leg, there is no harm in leaving the marks of the driving centre in the bottom of the leg as they will not be seen. There is no need to conceal the marks of the centre at the top either because you will need to form a spigot to fit the leg into the stool seat.

Turning

The maximum length for turning on the very smallest lathes will be reduced even further if you use a live centre. Some lathes are supplied with a mini four-pronged driving centre which will not really stand up to the task of turning a stool leg greater than 25mm (1in) in diameter, so for anything above this you will have to obtain a larger drive centre as an accessory. The diameter of

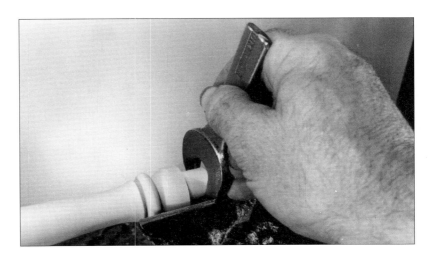

17 Sizing the spigot of a stool leg with a sharpened spanner

the spigot must be the same as that of the hole you drill in the stool seat to ensure a tight fit. Sizing can be done using the beading and parting tool and callipers, although the problem with this method is that the callipers can become maladjusted during use. A more accurate way to achieve regular spigot diameters is to use a spanner either as a measuring device or, by sharpening a bevel on one of the prongs, as a cutting device (photo 17).

When you have worked out a design for one stool leg you will need to record it so that you can make the others the same shape. Use a piece of hardboard cut to shape which can be held against the work while it is on the lathe or, if it is a fairly small stool leg, you can use a profile gauge composed of steel or plastic rods which slide in a centre sleeve and stay in place by friction. I normally use callipers and a rule. The dimensions of any square sectioned pieces can be marked off with pencil lines and a set square. After roughing the rounded sections to a cylinder, mark the positions of the main features by measuring with a ruler and holding a pencil against the work while it is rotating. Callipers and/or spanners can then be used to measure the maximum and minimum diameters at key places along the length as you turn.

If you can shape the stool legs so that they are all exactly the same length and your floor is flat, make a stool with four legs. If not, make one with three. If there are clear differences between the finished legs, make the stool top bigger so that they are further apart and therefore more difficult to compare.

18 The finished stool leg on the lathe

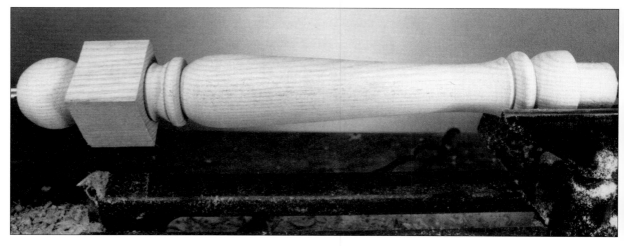

One of the most difficult things to master in spindle turning is leaving a square section while shaping the rest of the blank so that there is a crisp shoulder at the junction, as in photo 18. This is firstly because you must start by cutting into the corners of the wood with little support from the bevel of the tool. Secondly, the rest can very easily catch the square edges if you are not careful about stopping the lathe before adjusting it. Once damaged, these edges are impossible to restore. It can also be painful to the fingers if you accidentally touch the edges of the wood while they are in motion. I used a skew slicing cut to form the square section on the stool leg shown in photo 18, but if you find this difficult, it is possible to cut it with a very good, sharp saw. You can then turn up to the saw marks. When using a skew chisel, it is advisable to start cutting some distance from the area designated for the square section. This is because if you force the tool in, the grain may be distorted or the fibres raised and you want this to take place away from the shoulder. Remove the bulk well away from the line and then gradually slice towards it with the point of the skew. This means that you do not need to make deep cuts at the line, which eliminates tear out.

You will probably find it difficult to turn a long, flowing curve using the short rests supplied with the very smallest lathes. It is worth investing in a longer rest which you will not need to keep moving up and down the full extent of the curve.

Stool top

None of the lathes featured in this book are suitable for turning a stool top larger than 305mm (12in) in diameter. Unless you want to restrict your top to this size, it will be necessary to cut it to shape with a saw, finishing with a plane. If you do turn the top and only have a faceplate to fix it to the lathe, the easiest way to prevent the screw holes from showing is to plane the bottom and use this as the surface against the faceplate.

You will need to drill holes in the top for the spigots (mortises for the tenons) and you may want to do these at some other angle than 90 degrees. This procedure can either be done on a pillar drill or you can make a jig to work with your electric or hand drill.

Candlestick

TIMBER

65mm (2½in) x 65mm x 150mm (6in) of any hardwood, preferably with an interesting grain

LATHE SPEED

1330–2250 rpm

CHUCKING

Between centres

Turning

One method of making a candlestick is to turn a 12mm (½in) spigot at each end of a blank. Shape the candlestick so that it flares out at the top to catch the running wax and make sure that it is wide enough to hold a candle. The top of the candlestick should be at the tailstock so that the hole for the candle can be partly hollowed out as part of the turning process (Fig. 14a–c); there is only the centre point to circumnavigate at this end. Use a cranked tool made either from an Allen key ground with a square end with a flat on top or from an old chisel (as in Fig. 13 page 37). Naturally, you cannot remove all of the wood from the hole at this stage. It is better to establish the sides of the hole and only when you have finished turning the rest of the candlestick, reduce the spigot inside the hole as much as you dare. Clean off by hand after removing the candlestick from the lathe.

19 Group of candlesticks

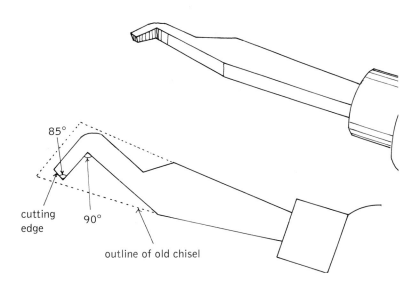

85°

cutting
edge

90°

outline of old chisel

*Fig. 13 Cranked, skew-ended
scraper made from a chisel*

Alternatively, it is possible to use an 18mm (¾in) or 25mm (1in) drill bit (these are the two standard candle diameters) to bore the hole for the candle. This can either be done before turning the candlestick (when this end can be supported by the live centre) or afterwards.

Next insert a piece of copper pipe in the hole to prevent the candle from scorching the wood as it burns down. This is best cut to length with a pipe cutter, which leaves the end nicely rolled over, but it can also be done with a hacksaw. It is not absolutely essential to have a metal insert but, in addition to protecting the wood, it also disguises the rough hole made by the drill.

Fig. 14a–c Candlestick

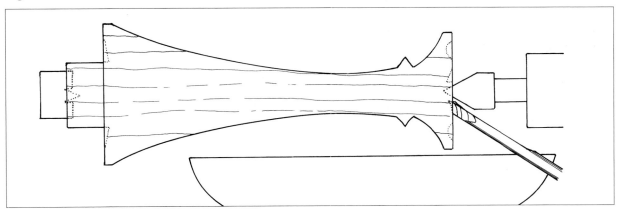

a Hollowing the candle recess with a spindle gouge

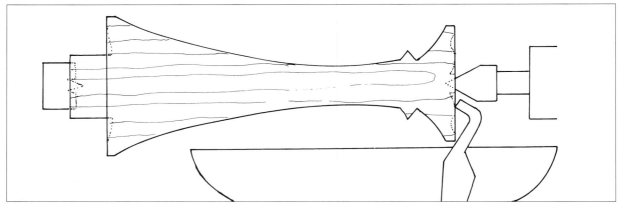

b Starting to hollow the candle recess with cranked, skew-ended scraper

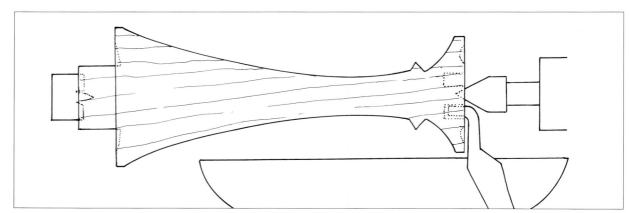

c Finishing the candle recess

Design tip

If you decide to make a pair of candlesticks, ensure that the wood used for each has a similar grain, although this can be difficult if it is exceptionally wild. Shape the first candlestick working to measurements which will be easy to duplicate – the width of a certain tool for example might be taken as one of the dimensions.

Lightpull

TIMBER

22mm (⁷/₈in) x 22mm x 32mm (1¹/₄in) of any type of hardwood for a small lightpull or 35mm (1³/₈in) x 35mm x 57mm (2¹/₄in) for a larger one

LATHE SPEED

2250 rpm

CHUCKING

Between centres

20 Ash lightpull [inset]
21 Group of lightpulls

Design

A lightpull should be easy to grip with a hole down the centre through which a typical lightpull cord can be inserted. In order to conceal the knot at the end of the cord a recess wider than the diameter of this hole should be formed at the base of the lightpull.

Turning

Cut a blank of the suggested length on the bandsaw and drill a short hole approximately 10mm (³/₈in) deep in one end using a 10mm centre drill bit. Then, using a 4mm (⁵/₃₂in) drill bit, bore another hole in the centre of the existing one that goes the whole length of the lightpull (Fig. 15). Alternatively, use the drill bit supplied by Reg Sherwin that does the whole job in one operation.

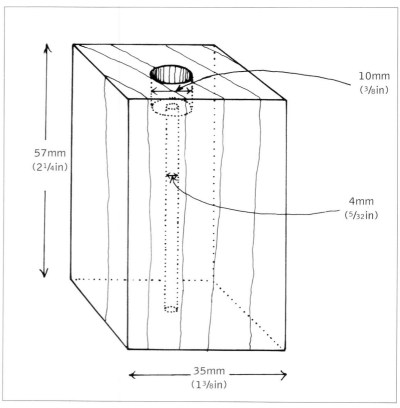

10mm
(³/₈in)

57mm
(2¹/₄in)

4mm
(⁵/₃₂in)

35mm
(1³/₈in)

Fig. 15 Lightpull blank – drilled

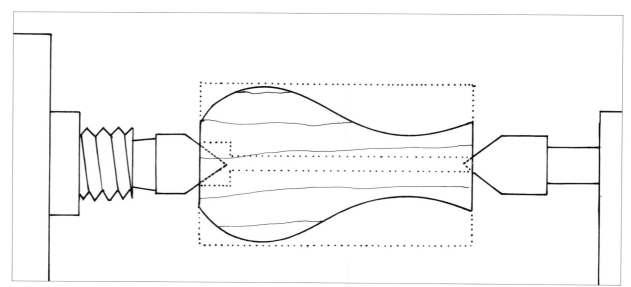

Fig. 16 Lightpull supported between dead centre in headstock and revolving centre in tailstock

You can hold the bit in a drill press or in an electric drill. It is also possible to use a Jacob's chuck, holding the blank by hand against the drill bit or to hold the blank in a four-jaw chuck and hold the bit in a chuck in the tailstock.

After drilling the hole in the blank, mount it between a dead centre in the headstock end of the lathe and a revolving centre in the tailstock end (Fig. 16). Provided the tension between the two points is maintained, there will be sufficient friction between the dead centre and the blank to keep the work rotating. (This is a technique much used by Reg Sherwin.)

The lightpull can then be roughed out with a gouge or skew chisel and shaped to your taste. It is important to finish the ends square, preferably using a slicing cut with the point of a skew. Finally, sand the lightpull and apply a suitable finish such as Craftese, which is a friction polish containing shellac. This provides the type of gloss finish which, in this case, tends to be more popular than a matt, oiled surface.

Lace Bobbin

TIMBER

10mm (³⁄₈in) x 10mm x 150mm (6in) of any straight- and close-grained hardwood

LATHE SPEED

2250 rpm +

CHUCKING

To turn the timber between centres requires some support at the head-stock end to prevent the timber from flexing. This support can be given either by using a commercial lace bobbin chuck or a Jacob's chuck or, in the case of those lathes which have hollow spindles and morse tapers, you can use the spindle hol-low as a chuck. To turn a run of lace bobbins, insert the bobbin blanks between centres and turn the end of the bobbin at the tailstock end to fit the chuck or morse taper.

22 Roughing out a bobbin blank on a Tyme Little Gem

Design

Lace bobbins vary according to the type of lace and the lace-maker's preference. Information about the different designs can be found in my earlier book *Turning Boxes and Spindles: Step-by-Step*, also published by Batsford, and in *Pillow Lace and Bobbins* by Jeffrey Hopewell, published by Shire Publications Ltd.

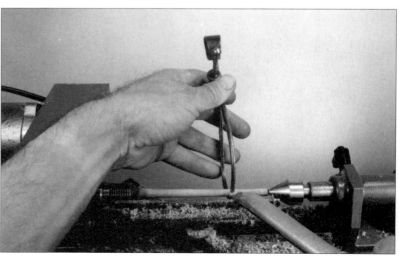

23 Measuring the thickness of a bobbin with callipers

Turning

Insert the blank in the chuck and rough turn it using either a skew chisel or a gouge so that it is circular in cross-section and roughly 6mm (¼in) in diameter (photo 22). Use either callipers or a spanner for sizing (photo 23).

When turning spindles, particularly with fine work such as lace bobbins, start turning at the tailstock end and then work towards the headstock. The reason for this is that the power is transmitted through the body of the work and if you make it too fine at the headstock end it is likely to break. First of all, mark off the neck and body. Form the thistle using either the point of a skew or a gouge. Cut the neck to the correct diameter (4mm (⅛in)) and then proceed to shape the body using the point of the skew or gouge to form beads and coves. A planing cut from the skew will make the long curves smooth. Finally, sand and finish the lace bobbin and part off.

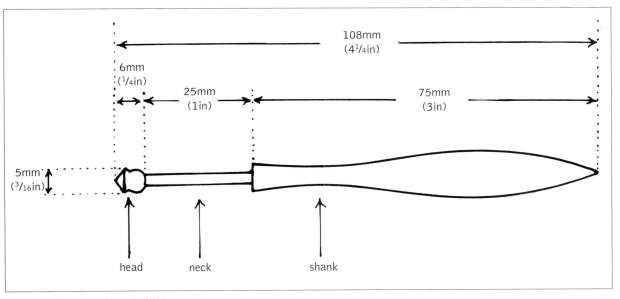

Fig. 17 Honiton lace bobbin

Niddy-Noddy

A niddy-noddy is most commonly used by hand-spinners for winding wool into skeins in preparation for washing and dyeing. It is comprised of a piece of dowelling with a fixed cross-piece at one end. The other end of the dowelling fits into a handle (Fig. 18). Another cross-piece then slides up and down the dowelling and is held in position by a wood screw. This is generally used at right angles to the fixed cross-piece and the distance between the two is varied according to requirements.

Turning

The thin piece is too long to be turned on the smallest lathes and there is little point in trying to do so when it is readily available in the form of dowelling. The diameter of dowelling tends to vary slightly so it is best to buy it before making the other parts of the niddy-noddy so that you can select your drill bit accordingly. The dowelling is inserted into a hole drilled in the end of the handle. It makes sense to drill this before you start to turn so that you can centre the handle accurately by inserting the live centre in the hole made by the drill.

The end cross-piece is simply turned and then drilled at right

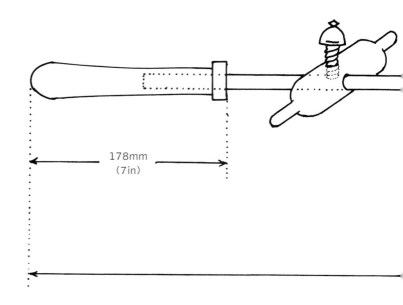

178mm
(7in)

Fig. 18 Niddy-noddy

there is no need for any great accuracy. It is then glued in place. The position of the hole in the moveable cross-piece can also be judged by eye although there is the added complication of the screw. The screw and threaded hole are best formed with a tap and die specifically made for wood and these can be bought from woodturning accessory shops. It is best to use boxwood for the screw but any really hard, fine-grained wood will do. Turn the screw section to the diameter of the top of the screw thread. Then turn the knob so it is circular in cross-section, prior to changing it into a flat-sided head using a sanding disc. The thread is formed by holding the screw in a vice and rotating the thread cutter around it. This must be done in very short rotations to prevent a build-up of wood in the cutter. The blade of the thread cutter must be kept extremely sharp and you should work gently to avoid breaking the timber at the top of the threads. Drill the hole for the screw in the bottom cross-piece to the minimum diameter of the troughs in the screw thread. Use the tap by inserting it in a vice and, as with the die, rotate the cross-piece around it in short rotations in order not to place stress on the wood.

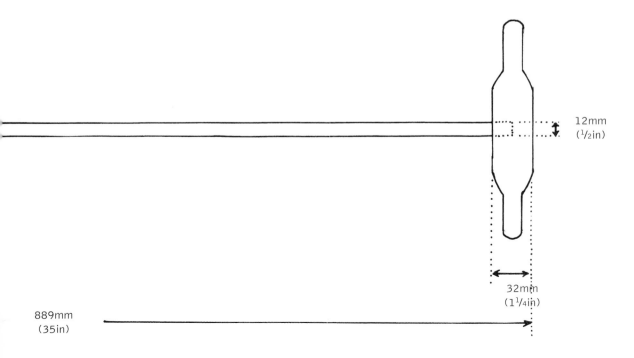

12mm
(¹/₂in)

32mm
(1¹/₄in)

889mm
(35in)

Lazy Kate

A Lazy Kate is a device used by hand spinners for plying wool. Spinning wheels are supplied with the bobbins held by the cross-members and it is best to use these rather than attempt to turn them yourself because they are made to the exact dimensions for use with the spinning wheel. The spinner fills up to three bobbins of wool and, when full, places them on the Lazy Kate and passes the three strands through the spinning wheel in order to produce a thicker, plied wool. The Lazy Kate should simply allow the bobbins to rotate and the whole structure should be sufficiently heavy not to be pulled across the floor too easily during the plying process. As with the niddy-noddy, I recommend using dowelling for the rods.

24 Lazy Kate

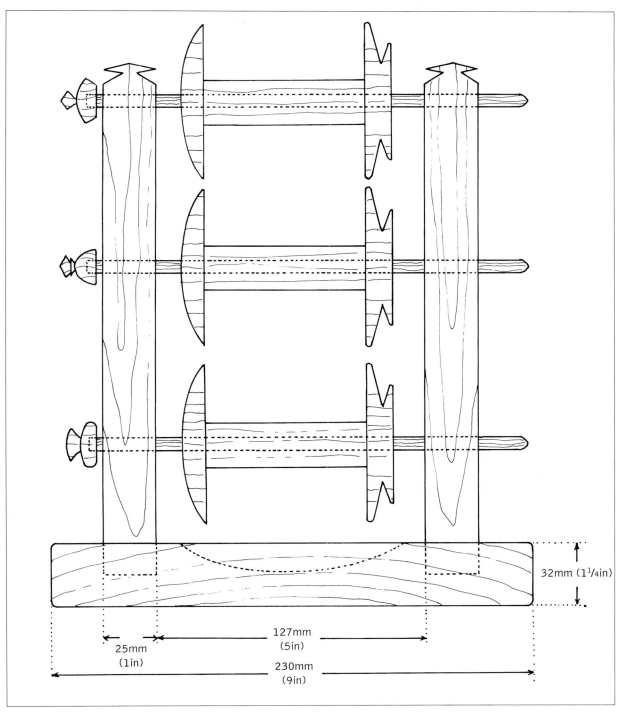

Fig. 19 Lazy Kate

Design

In the case of the Lazy Kate illustrated, the base is circular, but as it is about 230mm (9in) in diameter, users of the very smallest lathes may find it difficult to make. There is no reason therefore why the base should not be square in section or cut into a circular shape on a bandsaw. The Lazy Kate shown here has a recess in the top centre of the base. Largely a decorative feature, it also serves to collect any stray pieces of wool as they fall. I used ash for this project, but most hardwoods are suitable.

Turning

It is relatively simple to turn the base if your lathe is large enough. First attach the faceplate to what will become the bottom of the base in order to make the top and sides smooth. Then reverse the base on to the faceplate and hold it in place with screws inserted where the holes for the uprights will be drilled. This ensures that no screw holes are visible on the top.

The uprights are also simply turned – those shown in photo 24 are straight cylinders. You can turn spigots on the ends so that the shoulders of the uprights conceal the edges of the holes in the base into which they fit.

The method of turning the knobs on the ends of the rods (Fig. 20a–c) is perhaps the most interesting aspect of this exercise because some of the principles involved are applicable to other projects. Use a piece of wood which is sufficient to turn all three at once taking into account the spigot at the headstock end and the width of your parting tool plus an extra piece for truing off the end at the tailstock.

Fig. 20a shows the spigot turned at the headstock end, the two gaps made by the parting tool and the end being cleaned off with a slicing cut from a skew. The driving centre is then replaced either by a three- or four-jaw chuck; a cup chuck made of wood mounted on a faceplate or even a Jacob's chuck. This enables you to use a drill bit held in a Jacob's chuck mounted in the tailstock (Fig. 20b) to make the hole in the knob. It is important to use a brad point drill for this because the point of an engineer's pattern twist bit tends to wander as it is inserted. Once the hole is made

Fig. 20a–c Knobs for Lazy Kate

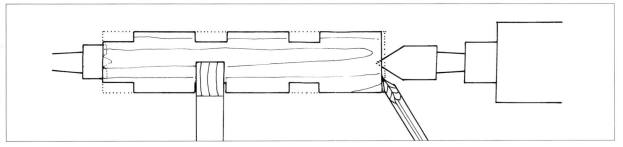

a Preparing blank between centres for three-jaw chuck

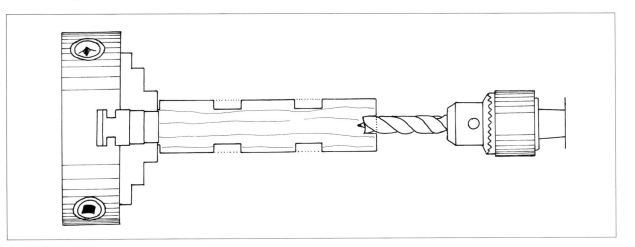

b Drilling hole

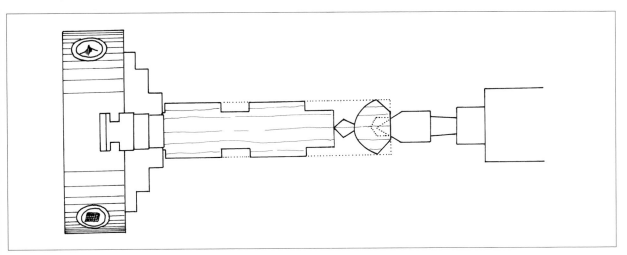

c Outside shaped and about to be parted off

sufficiently deep to grip the rod, the drill bit and Jacob's chuck can be replaced with a revolving centre which can be inserted in the hole to facilitate the shaping of the knob (Fig. 20c). I have made three differently shaped knobs in this instance simply for decorative purposes.

Spinning Top

TIMBER

40mm (1¹/₂in) x 40mm x 100mm
(4in) of any straight- and close-
grained hardwood

LATHE SPEED

2250 rpm

Design

Spinning top shapes vary enormously but the ones that spin longest do so because of the flywheel effect (see photo 25 and Fig. 22a–c). This is achieved by making the outside of the flywheel thicker than the inside. The stem of the spinning top should be easy to twist between finger and thumb. Apart from these criteria, there is ample scope for you to personalize the top.

25 Oak spinning top with nail insert

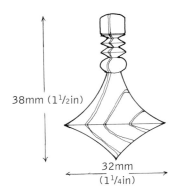

38mm (1¹/₂in)

32mm
(1¹/₄in)

Fig. 21 Spinning top

Turning

A spinning top must be supported at one end while being turned so that the point upon which it rotates can be made perfectly true. In order to do this, the blank should be roughed out between centres (Fig. 22a) and a spigot turned on one end to fit into a chuck or into the headstock spindle. The top should be finished using the tool rather than sandpaper. Abrasives will tend to render the shape asymmetrical due to differential sanding and this will affect the way the top spins.

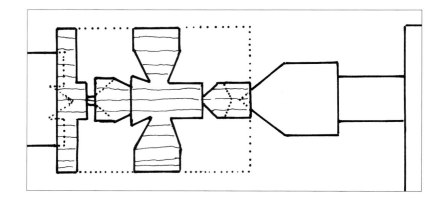

Fig. 22a–c Spinning top with nail point

a Shaping between centres

Turning a top with a nail point

For a really hard, long-lasting and sharp point on a spinning top, metal is the best substance. A metal point can be provided easily by using a nail, which should be knocked into the base, point first, and then removed (Fig. 22b). Cut off the head of the nail and

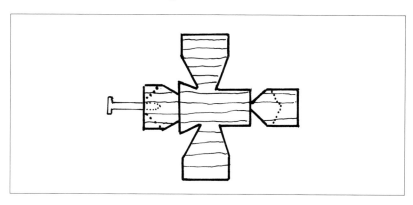

b After parting off, insert nail

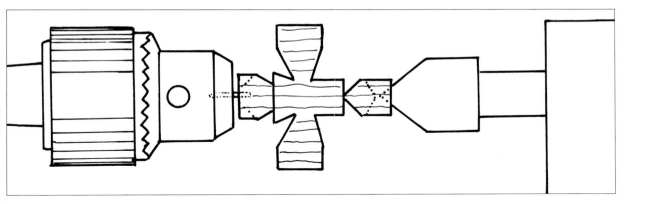

c Shaping both points: top supported by Jacob's chuck gripping nail

give it a screwdriver or chisel end by grinding it. Put it back into the hole, chisel end first, so that the top turns on the point of the nail. If you apply some superglue before re-inserting it, the nail will stay firmly in place. The blank can now be supported by the nail in a Jacob's chuck to allow both ends of the spinning top to be turned (Fig. 22c). It is not advisable to use a nail point if the top is likely to be used by children.

Hollowing Projects

The projects in this section involve hollowing into end grain. The techniques used are covered very comprehensively in my second book, *Turning Boxes and Spindles: Step-by-Step*.

With this type of project, the grain runs parallel to the bed of the lathe and the work needs to be at one end only so that the other end can be hollowed. To facilitate this, the blank is first roughed out between centres and one end trued up and turned to fit your chuck. If you do this at the tailstock end you will avoid catching the tool on the forks of the driving centre.

The simplest and cheapest chuck to use is a home-made, wooden cup chuck as seen in the pepper mill project Fig. 26c on page 73) but you can also use a three- or four-jaw or combination chuck in the compression mode. It is unwise to use a faceplate because screwing into end grain does not provide a satisfactory grip.

Hollowing end grain is not easy. If you try cutting from the outside in as with a side grain bowl, you will find the wood feels very hard and tends to cause the tool to judder. Shavings are almost impossible to produce. To turn with the grain requires cutting from the inside out so you need to drill a hole down the centre of the work and work from the inside of this hole. This hole can be made with a drill but I do the whole operation with a spindle gouge with a ground back side (Fig. 2 page 18). Set the rest so that if the gouge is held horizontally it will cut exactly through the centre of the work. Push the tool carefully straight into the middle with the central part of the tool doing the cutting. When the hole is well established, the depth can be measured on the side of the item by using the thumb as a stop, inserting the tool until the thumbnail touches the top.

Hold the tool flute upwards, rotate it anticlockwise about five degrees, and hollow with the side which faces outwards. Pivot the tool on the centre of the rest by holding it down with the finger or thumb but keep it horizontal throughout the whole process (see photo 10 page 17). The cut starts inside the hole near the top and is enlarged in width and depth as the material is removed. Because the bevel does not rub in this cut, the margins for error are small but with practice the wood can be removed expeditiously.

If the walls of the piece are thin, you can use the thumb to control the tool and the fingers on the outside to absorb the vibrations – though this takes practice. This cut tends not to leave a very smooth finish and I usually need to make a finishing fine cut with a sharp scraper before sanding inside. In the case of a straight-sided vessel you can use a square-ended scraper, but when the vessel has a rounded internal profile you will need a domed one.

Egg Cup

TIMBER

75mm (3in) x 75mm x 100mm (4in) of yew will make two egg cups

LATHE SPEED

1330 rpm

CHUCKING

Fig. 23a–c shows the method of making an unusual type of egg cup mounted in a cup chuck but it is possible to use a chuck in the compression mode instead

Design

This egg cup is made in the form of a ring rather than a full cup. This is because egg cups tend to support most eggs (due to their size variability) on a single line of latitude rather than the whole surface of a hemisphere. In other words, as it is not possible to turn a cup that corresponds perfectly with the shape of every egg, you might just as well make a ring.

26 Yew egg cup

Turning

Turn a spigot at the tailstock end to fit the cup chuck. Fig. 23a shows the inside of the egg cup hollowed. The parting tool is used to turn part way towards the hollowed section. Fig. 23b shows the outside of the egg cup after it has been shaped either by a spindle gouge or skew chisel.

Fig. 23a–c Egg cup

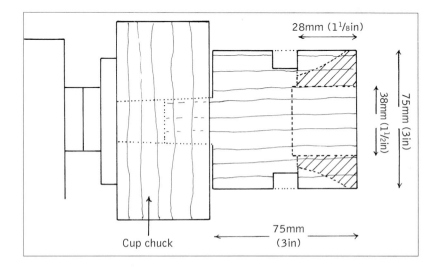

a After hollowing form the cove with a parting tool

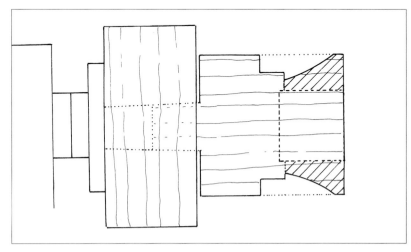

b Shape the outside

The next stage is to sand the sides, bottom and inside of the egg cup which can then be parted off by removing the remaining shoulder of wood with a skew chisel (Fig. 23c). This should leave

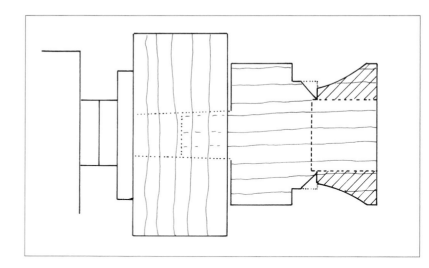

c Cut the top of the egg cup with a skew

a sufficiently good finish on the top surface of the egg cup not to require any further sanding. If you are unable to get a sufficiently good finish from the tool on the top surface, reverse the egg cup on to a tapered piece of wood which is held either in the cup chuck or between centres and sized to fit the inside diameter of the egg cup. If it is tapered it will accommodate several different sizes.

Napkin Ring

The napkin ring is made in much the same way as the egg cup except that the sides are parallel and can be ornamented if you wish. The size of the blank will depend on the diameter of the napkin ring required and on how many you wish to make from the same piece.

27 Ash napkin ring

Candleholder

TIMBER

75mm (3in) x 75mm x 125mm (5in)
of lacewood or similar timber

LATHE SPEED

1330 rpm

CHUCKING

If you use a cup chuck, combination
chuck, faceplate or single screw
chuck, this is a simple end grain hollowing exercise (see page 54). The
candleholder can also be turned
between centres using the method
described below

Turning

A pair of candleholders can be turned between centres if you do
not have a chuck. Use a cranked, skew-ended scraper to form the
shallow hole for the candle. If you want to make a recess at one
end for a 50mm (2in) candle and a recess at the other end for a
25mm (1in) or 19mm (³⁄₄in) candle, you will need a pair of skew-
ended scrapers with the cutting edge on opposite sides. The
advantage of using this method to turn your candleholders is that
you will be able to match the two very easily and even change the
design as you go along if you make a mistake. If you are going to
make recesses at both ends, and this is by no means essential,
leave approximately 25mm (1in) between the candleholders to
allow each one to be hollowed out.

28 Lacewood candleholder

Pencil Pot

TIMBER

64mm (2¹/₂in) x 64mm x 100mm
(4in) of brown oak or similar timber

LATHE SPEED

1330–2250 rpm

CHUCKING

Use a cup chuck, combination chuck,
single screw chuck or three- or four-
jaw chuck (see page 54)

Design

It is quite a challenge to make a simple pot shape aesthetically
pleasing. I made this one to the same dimensions as a jam jar,
relieving the straightness of each side by giving it a slight inward
curve. A bead at the bottom (formed with a gouge, skew or fluted
parting tool), counterbalanced by two smaller beads at the top,
lends interest and definition. The pot can be finished off with a
pyrographed label if you wish – this will show up better on a
lighter coloured wood than brown oak.

29 Brown oak pencil pot

Box

Boxes should be hollowed from end grain (i.e. the grain will run from top to bottom of the finished item) rather than being made with the grain running from side to side – this ensures greater stability. The size of the blank will vary depending on the sort of wood you are using and the size of your lathe. The dimensions of the blank shown in Fig. 24a and b are 50mm (2in) x 50mm x 125mm (5in).

30 Group of boxes 40mm (1⁹⁄₁₆in) and 3mm (¹⁄₈in) in diameter

Turning

Mount the blank between centres and shape the end at the tail-stock so that it will fit into the compression jaws of a combination chuck. The dotted lines in Fig. 24a indicate the eventual shape of the box within the blank. If it is turned as shown, the grain should run fairly naturally from the top into the body.

Fig. 24a–h Box
a Preparing the blank for the chuck

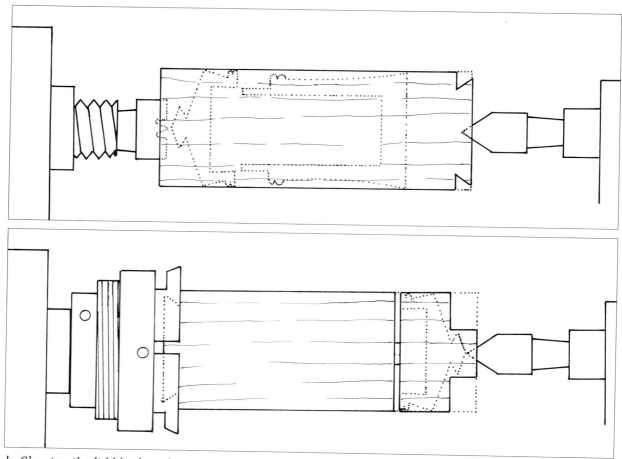

b Shaping the lid blank and parting off

Fig. 24b shows the blank mounted in the combination chuck with the tailstock brought up to support the work while the spigot is turned at the tailstock end. Part off the lid using the thinnest parting tool available. This may be a purpose-made tool (Fig. 4 page 18) or you can use a hacksaw while the wood is rotating slowly on the lathe, providing you wear full protective gear.

After parting off, there are two ways of hollowing the inside of the lid. The first method is to mount it in a three- or four-jaw chuck (Fig. 24c). The second method is to mount the lid in a tapered hole turned in the body of the box (Fig. 24d). When you hollow the inside of the lid you should make the sides parallel or very slightly overhung. It is vital that the sides do not taper inwards or the lid will tend to come off too easily.

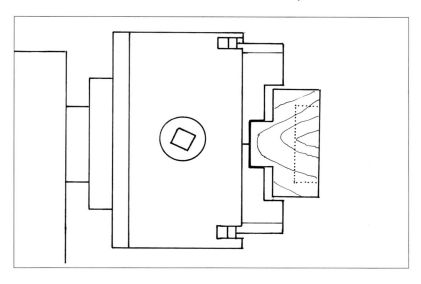

c *Hollowing the lid (method 1)*

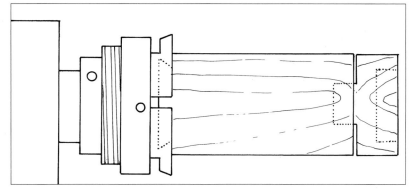

d *Hollowing the lid (method 2)*

Fig. 24e shows the body of the box in the combination chuck. First, turn the lip to accept the lid of the box. Start by turning a short spigot approximately the same diameter as the inside of the lid so that if you make it too small (so the lid is too loose) you can remove the spigot and start again without wasting too much wood. When the lid is a tight fit you can extend the length of the spigot to the desired size of lip. It is not necessary to make the lip a perfect fit for the lid at this stage. Indeed, it is actually better if it is fractionally too tight. The reason for this is that as you hollow out the inside of the box at the next stage, the wood heats up and if it then shrinks the lid will become too loose.

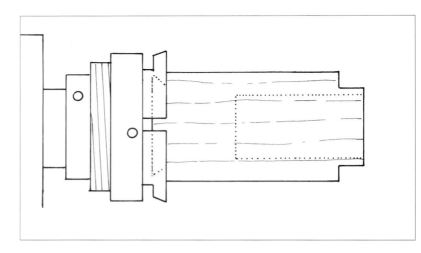

e Hollowing the body of the box

Hollow out the inside of the box with a spindle gouge and fit the lid as shown in Fig. 24f. The outside shape of the box can then be turned according to your design. In Fig. 24f you can see the two beads where the lid meets the body of the box. This is not simply for decorative purposes but it does also help to disguise any difference between the grain of the lid and that of the body. In addition, it also helps you to grip and remove the lid as do the sloping sides.

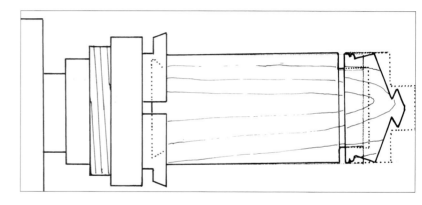

f Shaping the outside of the lid

After turning the outside of the lid to shape, pare the lip down carefully using the beading and parting tool in order to make it a perfect fit. This should not be too tight – although it is nice to make the lid pop when you pull it off, the wood may well contract after you have finished it in which case it will be almost impossible to remove. Sand the inside of the lid but do not touch the sides or you will affect the fit. Oil and wax the inside of the lid and the inside of the bottom of the box.

Turn the outside of the box to complement the design of the lid (Fig. 24g) and you can then part off the whole piece. Leave plenty of wood at the bottom of the box because if the base is too

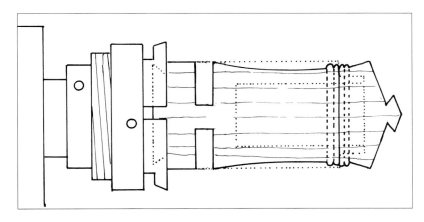

g *Shaping the outside of the box*

thin, the short grain fibres may be pulled out in the centre as you part off. It is possible to part off most of the way using a beading and parting or parting tool. Then smooth off the bottom using a skew or one-sided skew. It should require very little sanding afterwards but you will get a better finish if you can turn the bottom of the box after reverse chucking it. To do this use the stub of wood left in the combination chuck as a push-fit chuck by turning a spigot on it to accept the inside of the box (Fig. 24h). Very little turning is required to get rid of the pip left on the bottom of the box so the spigot should not be very long. If by any chance you make it too small, it is possible to put a piece of tissue paper or rag over the spigot in order to make the fit a good one. With some skill, you can even hold the bottom section of the box in position on a loose-fitting spigot with the left hand while turning off the bottom with the right.

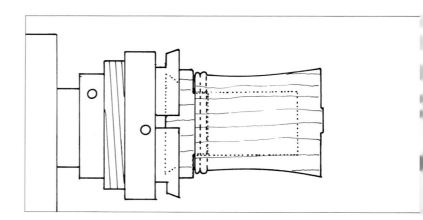

h Finishing off the base

Finally, lightly sand the exterior of the box and apply oil and wax.

Elm Cruet Set

TIMBER

44mm (1³/₄in) x 44mm x 150mm (6in) of elm for two cruets

ACCESSORIES

You will need rubber bungs and steel shaker tops for the designs shown in photos 31 and 32. These can be obtained from sundries suppliers

LATHE SPEED

2250 rpm

CHUCKING

See page 54

Turning

Mount the blank between centres and rough out, forming a spigot at the tailstock end to fit a chuck. Then mount the blank in the chuck, truing up the projecting end. Measure the blank and put a mark half-way along its length, leaving a space between the two sections for parting off. In this example the two cruets are approximately 64mm (2¹/₂in) long with a gap in between of 6mm (¹/₄in) for parting off.

Pepper pot

True up the end and mark on it the diameter of the steel shaker top. Form a hole right through the centre of the blank using a spindle gouge or Forstner bit of the same diameter as the rubber bung. The shaker top is accommodated by hollowing out the top

31 Elm cruet set

to the appropriate width and depth (Fig. 25a). You can then widen the hole inside to increase the capacity of the pepper pot. Now shape the external contours.

Fig. 25a–b Cruet set

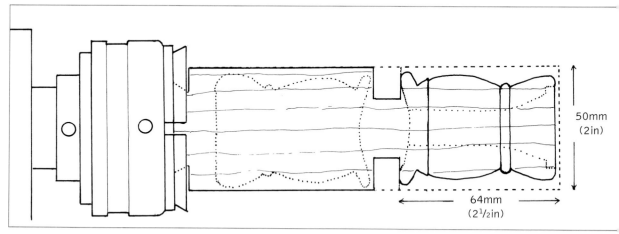

50mm (2in)

64mm (2½in)

a The pepper pot shaped and hollowed to accommodate bung and top

Sand and finish the pepper pot and then part off with the skew, making sure that the bottom is sufficiently concave to allow for the depth of the bung.

Salt-cellar

Hollow the outside end to the depth of the outer flange of the rubber bung so that this does not project below the base of the salt-cellar. Using a pair of dividers, mark the diameter of the bung.

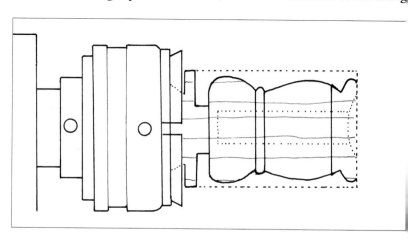

b Pepper pot parted off. Salt-cellar shaped and hollowed to accommodate bung

(in this case 16mm (5/8in)) on to the base of the salt-cellar and remove a corresponding amount of wood using a spindle gouge (Fig. 25b). Make sure that the hole is only just wide and deep enough (6mm (1/4in)) to accommodate the bung, but if you wish you can expand it as you work further inside to increase the capacity of the salt-cellar. Continue hollowing almost until you reach the other end. You need only sand the inside of the hole if the surface is very rough.

Check the depth of the cavity against the overall length of the salt-cellar to ensure that there is neither too much nor too little wood at the top of the salt-cellar. Then start a right-angled parting cut with the skew, level with the top of the salt-cellar. The other side of the parting cut should be at an oblique angle to allow you to work the skew into the gap. Now shape the external surfaces to match the design of the pepper pot. Sand and finish the salt-cellar and then part off using a slicing cut with the skew to leave a good, clean surface on top. Finally, drill a fine hole in the top of the salt-cellar through which to pour the salt.

Cherry Cruet Set

For this project you need to obtain and season some branch wood approximately 50mm (2in) in diameter. The timber can only be used if it is without a pith and if it does not split during the seasoning process. The method of turning these salt and pepper pots is essentially the same as for the elm cruet set except that they are simply cylindrical in shape. The bark gives them an interesting textured appearance.

32 Bark-sided cruet set

Oak Cruet Set

Cruet sets can be made to an infinite number of designs. This particular set was made to complement a large pepper mill. The salt and pepper pots are quite simply two spherical boxes with upper and lower halves. Fit the lids in exactly the same way as for the box on page 63. Obviously, they need to fit quite tightly in this case so they do not come apart too easily, spilling their contents everywhere. Either drill small holes at the top for the salt and pepper or, as shown here, drill holes for the pepper and simply put a scoop in the other pot to serve sea salt.

33 Spherical, oak cruet set

Pepper Mill

TIMBER

Use a straight-grained, relatively soft timber such as sycamore, lacewood or ash to facilitate the drilling operation. For this mill, I used a 114mm (4$^1/_2$in) mechanism. The blank is 57mm (2$^1/_4$in) x 57mm x 150mm (6in)

ACCESSORIES

The pepper mill needs a grinding mechanism, available from suppliers of woodturning accessories

Turning

The most efficient way to turn a pepper mill is to hollow the inside of the bottom section with a Forstner or saw tooth bit but, if you only intend to make one pepper mill and do not want to buy such a bit, it is possible to use normal end grain hollowing techniques. If you do use a bit, I suggest that you practise the drilling technique on a piece of scrap wood before you start, partly to perfect it but also because it is crucial to get the size of the hole right in relation to the spigots on either end of the pepper mill top and you can only do this by making a hole first.

34 Lacewood pepper mill

Once you have established the size of the hole made by the bit (25mm (1in) in diameter is a useful size), mount the blank between centres and turn spigots at the ends of what will be the top (Fig. 26a). Then part off the top.

Fig. 26a–g Pepper mill

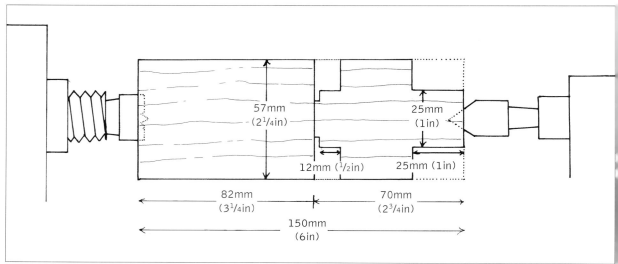

a Preparing top to fit base and parting off

To use a drill bit to bore the hole in the lower section of the pepper mill, first mount the bit in a Jacob's chuck in the headstock. Next, bring up the lower section held against the tailstock, start the lathe at the lowest possible speed and drill half way along (Fig. 26b). Take care not to go right through the bottom so that the drill bit comes into contact with the live centre as that will blunt the point. It is important when boring a hole with a drill

b Hollowing with Forstner bit

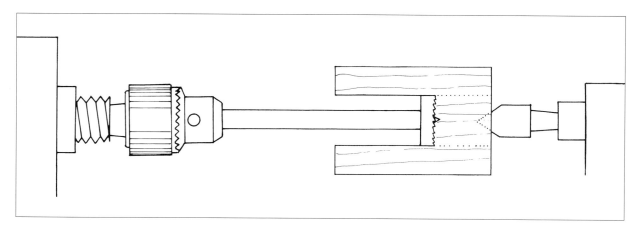

bit that you very frequently remove the bit from the hole to clear the detritus. If this is allowed to build up behind the drill, you may find that you are in the embarrassing position of having to drill the detritus out to remove the drill bit.

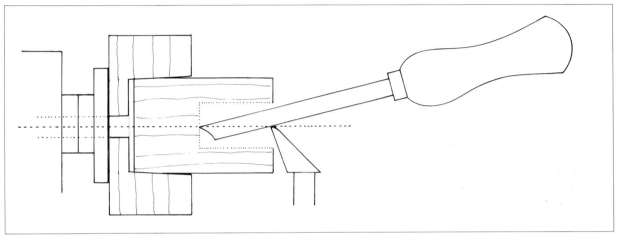

*c Hollowing with square-
ended scraper*

In order to finish the hole, the lower section of the pepper mill must be reversed so that the bit can be used. This can be facilitated by turning a plug to fit in the base of the mill, which can then be supported by the tailstock. Alternatively, mount the lower section of the pepper mill in a wooden cup chuck (you will need to do this in order to hollow with a scraper if you do not have a drill bit (Fig. 26c)) and the bit can be held in the tailstock while the headstock rotates. You could also mount the mill in one of the combination chucks if the end has been turned to fit the compression mode. As you can see in Fig. 26c, there is a hole in the base of the cup chuck through which the knock-out bar of the lathe can be pushed to remove the body of the pepper mill should it stick.

After drilling the hole through the body of the pepper mill, the long spigot of the top can be inserted into the hole. Then the hole for the central rod of the grinding mechanism can be formed using an appropriately sized bit in a Jacob's chuck in the tailstock (Fig. 26d). If your drill bit is not long enough to bore the hole in one go, the top of the pepper mill can be reversed in the bottom section so that the short spigot is in the hole and the drilling can be done through the long spigot.

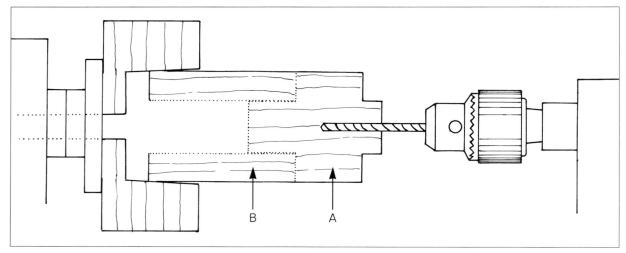

d Drilling top for grinding mechanism – top (A) supported in base (B)

The base of the pepper mill must then be turned to accommodate the grinding mechanism. This is done in two stages (shown in Fig. 26e) as the main part of the mechanism (which is 25mm (1in) in diameter) fits inside the hole but is held in place by a step and a cross bar which have a larger diameter. After drilling the top, the whole pepper mill must be mounted so that the outer shape of the top and bottom can be turned together. This can be done on a plug turned between centres or on a faceplate as in

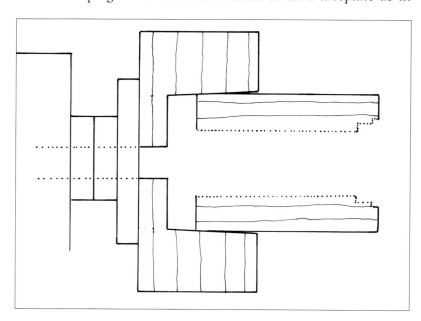

e Shaping the bottom of the base to accommodate the grinder

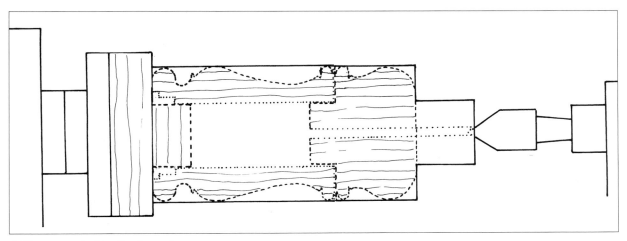

*f Top mounted in the base for
shaping the outer surfaces*

*35 Pepper mill top mounted in
base supported on a spigot
insert in a cup chuck*

Fig. 26f. Alternatively, if you are making a series of pepper mills, it is a good idea to turn such a plug with a 25mm (1in) spigot on it. This is so that the larger diameter of the plug fits in the cup chuck which you have used to turn the body of the pepper mill. The cup chuck can stay on the lathe for the whole operation once you have completed the first stage.

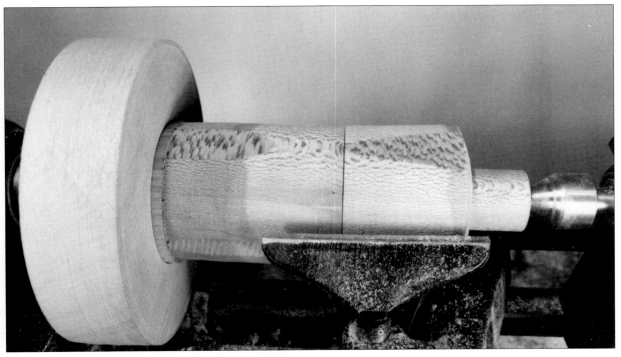

36 *Shaping the outside of the pepper mill*

37 *Parting off the pepper mill using a skew*

The turning of the outside of the pepper mill presents no particular problems (photos 35–7). Turn a bead on either side of the join where the top of the mill meets the bottom to disguise any lack of concentricity between the two sections. It is worth inserting the mechanism before parting off at the long spigot, in order to check that the length of the pepper mill is correct; if it is too short the knob that fits on the top threaded section of the rod will project too far out of the top and will not bear down firmly upon the top of the pepper mill. If this is the case then a decorative feature on the top is called for or you may be able to shorten the length of the shaft (at the bottom) and burr over the end so that it holds the grinding mechanism in place.

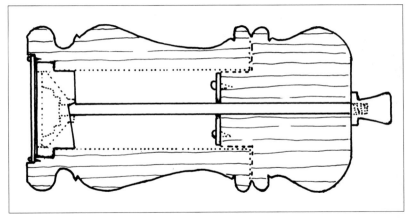

g *The finished pepper mill with the grinding mechanism in place*

Part Three: Furnishings for Dolls' Houses

When turning dolls' house pieces (the standard scale is $\frac{1}{12}$th) the making process is not necessarily the same as it is for the full-size equivalents. For example, there is no reason to make a miniature platter with the grain running at right angles to the axis of the lathe and to use an expanding chuck on the base. You can choose a really dense hardwood, such as box or laburnum, and make the piece with the grain running parallel to the axis of the lathe. When viewed from the end, the grain will actually look very similar to that of a platter made with the grain running at right angles to the axis of the lathe. Try to use wood with a tight grain (box and holly are ideal) so that the piece is in proportion right down to the finest detail.

While a small lathe does not allow you to turn very big pieces of wood, a large, well-made lathe is suitable for turning miniatures because it will run very true. Similarly, full-size tools can be used for small work because, for the most part, only the point or cutting edge comes into play. Hence, platters and breadboards can be made with a 19mm ($\frac{3}{4}$in) skew chisel. But for certain techniques, particularly for hollowing, you will undoubtedly need some miniature or even a set of micro tools (see page 19). If you decide you want to specialise in turning dolls' house furnishings and other very small pieces, one of these sets of tools actually represents a much cheaper investment than a full-size collection. Another inexpensive but useful alternative is to make some of your own tools by shaping small pieces of metal, such as masonry nails, to your requirements.

Platters

The average dinner plate is normally 279mm (11in) across and therefore a dolls' house platter should be approximately 22mm (⁷⁄₈in) in diameter. You can make a range of platters in different sizes from a small blank roughly 50mm (2in) long. Turn the blank between centres, forming a spigot at one end so that it can be gripped in a chuck. When using a small lathe it is important not to allow the blank to project too far from the headstock as the bearings therein will be unable to support it. When the blank is in the chuck, the sides and end can be trued up using a slicing cut with a skew chisel, point downwards.

Form a shallow recess at one end of the blank by hollowing very gently because when working on end grain, dense woods do not allow for many mistakes. If you work carelessly, presenting the tool at the wrong angle, it will catch and damage the platter. Once you have shaped the top surface, the platter must be parted from the rest of the blank. You can use a very fine parting tool

38 Boxwood dolls' house platters; 22mm (⁷⁄₈in) and 13mm (¹⁄₂in) in diameter

39 *Parting off a platter using a one-sided skew*

40 *Two bowls and a bread-board*

made from a hacksaw blade for this. However, a much better finish will be achieved if a one-sided skew is used to shape the outer surface and to cut across the bottom of the platter (photo 39). By getting into a smaller space, a one-sided skew wastes less wood than either a traditional parting tool or a normal skew chisel.

Breadboards and Bowls

A breadboard is made in the same way as a platter except that it has a circular groove (formed with a gouge or nail) on the top surface instead of a recessed centre. Follow the same method for bowls too, but continue hollowing until you reach an appropriate depth. It is important to ensure that the thickness of the bowl is in proportion to its depth. A full-size salad bowl is usually 300mm (12in) in diameter, in which case the scaled-down version is naturally 25mm (1in) across.

Candlesticks

Miniature versions of the candlesticks shown on page 36 can be made in a Jacob's chuck to allow the recesses to be hollowed. These can be sized to accommodate tiny candles which are available from dolls' house suppliers. Since the candles are very rarely lit, it actually makes sense to make permanent ones out of an alternative substance. I use bone because it is very cheap and readily available.

It is best to use the shin bone of a cow for this purpose. To prepare it, first cut off the ends of the bone as shown in Fig. 27 and boil it until the marrow is soft. Take out the bone and then boil it again in fresh water with added washing soda to remove the fats which might otherwise turn rancid. The bone can now be cut easily on a bandsaw or with a hacksaw, which is more difficult. Small pieces of bone are best gripped in the Jacob's chuck. The candles should be roughly 2mm ($1/12$in) thick and 12mm ($1/2$in) long.

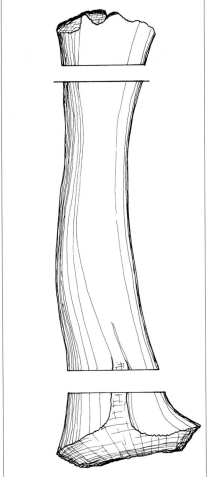

Fig. 27 Shin bone prepared for cutting and turning

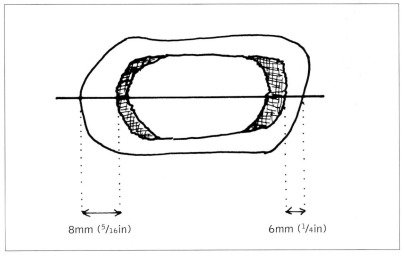

8mm ($5/16$in)   6mm ($1/4$in)

Tea Service

This particular tea service was not actually made to a ¹/₁₂th scale. It was conceived as a miniature rather than strictly for use in a dolls' house.

Cups and saucers

These are very straightforward as they are simply smaller versions of the platters and bowls shown on pages 79 and 80. To make the handles, first form some wooden rings by hollowing out a blank while supporting one end of it in a Jacob's chuck. Then part of the rings using a skew. After parting off, cut away a small section from each ring with a sharp knife. This will leave two flat surfaces for joining on to the cups. Hold the handle up to the cup to establish how much you need to pare away from the flat surfaces to make them fit neatly against the side of the cup. I use superglue (cyanoacrylate) to attach the handles to the cups.

41 Boxwood tea set on a tray
75mm (3in) in diameter

Teapot

The teapot itself is slightly more complicated than the cups and saucers (Fig. 28a and b). The pot is essentially a spherical box but the lid does not fit on the base in the same way as on pages 62–66. It simply sits in the hole and therefore does not need to be such a tight fit. Nor is it necessary to match up the grain patterns. The spout, however, is a more challenging shape to form. As you can see in Fig. 28b, the first stage when making the spout is to turn a symmetrical funnel-shaped piece. This can be done by mounting a piece of roughed-out wood in a Jacob's

Fig. 28a Dolls' house teapot

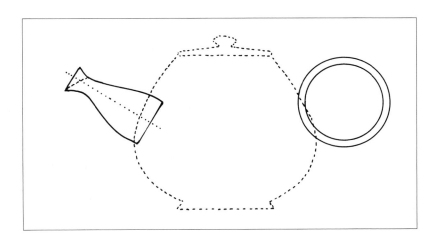

Fig. 28b Dolls' house teapot showing shapes from which spout and handle are formed

chuck. Shape the outside, making the fatter end the one furthest from the chuck and then hollow the inside using a very small gouge. It is rather difficult to hollow the ends of the spout where it flares out again but if this is not possible you can do all the hollowing you need by hand after parting off and removing the top part of the tip. Then shape the end of the spout where it fits on to the body of the teapot. In this example, I even drilled drainage holes where the spout joins the body of the teapot before gluing them together, but this is not strictly necessary.

Jug

Make the jug (Fig. 29) by turning a pot shape with a fairly thick rim. Form the spout by first lowering one section of the upper surface of the rim. Thin out the rim around this section so the spout remains wider and lower. On the side opposite the spout, indent the neck of the jug to accommodate the handle. The handle is made in the same way as for the cups and teapot.

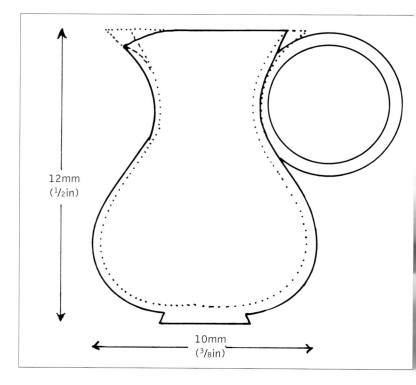

12mm
(1/2in)

10mm
(3/8in)

Fig. 29 Dolls' house milk jug

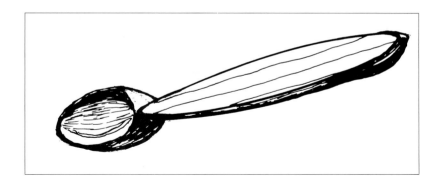

Fig. 30 Doll's house teaspoon

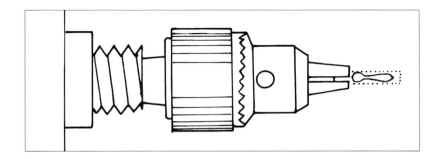

Fig. 31 Dolls' house teaspoon in Jacob's chuck

Spoons

The spoons (Fig. 30) are the most difficult aspect of this project. Start by turning the spoon shape shown in Fig. 31 and then flatten one side with a sanding disc. Use a tiny carving gouge to hollow out the bowl of the spoon. You could also use a small burr, which can be obtained for power carving, or a dentist's tool.

Sugar bowl and scoop

The bowl is turned in much the same way as an ordinary bowl except that, obviously, it is a fraction of the size. The scoop, on the other hand, is rather more complex. The blank should be mounted so that you can hollow out one end. Using a skew, shape the outside of the cup section before hollowing it out. Now shape the stem of the scoop. Very little sanding will be required and you can finish the scoop with oil and wax. Part off using the skew and then finish shaping the cup by removing part of the side with a piece of sandpaper.

Wine Bottle and Goblets

These goblets are made from bone (see page 81 for the method of preparing bone for turning). The shape of the bowl should be turned first and then hollowed with the point of a nail perhaps. Use a micro gouge or skew to turn the stem. If the bone is cut cleanly before it is turned, very little sanding is needed to achieve a smooth surface.

Turn the wooden wine bottle in a Jacob's chuck and drill a hole into it at the top for the stopper. Use a contrasting wood for the stopper just to show that it has been turned separately.

42 Wine bottle and goblets on a tray 25mm (1in) in diameter

Balusters

Balusters are turned in much the same way as a full-scale stool leg (see pages 33–34) except that you do need really sharp, small skews for the very fine detail. They are made from boxwood to a $^1/_{12}$th scale for a dolls' house staircase, so that assuming the average baluster is 800mm (32in) long by 50mm (2in) in diameter, the miniature version will be approximately 70mm (2$^3/_4$in) long by 4mm ($^5/_{32}$in) in diameter.

Prepare the wood straight and square before you start to turn. This can be done with a plane or a 125mm (5in) sanding disc on the lathe. Turn the balusters between centres, supporting one end in a Jacob's chuck to prevent any flexing that may be caused by the pressure exerted by the tailstock and a driving centre. This method of turning means that the blank should be 12mm ($^1/_2$in) longer than the eventual required length of the baluster.

43 Turning a boxwood baluster on a Tyme Little Gem. A magnifying glass makes the job easier

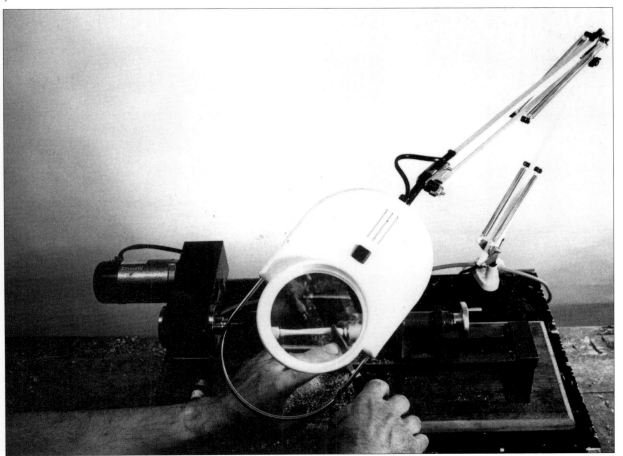

44 Finished baluster

For objects this small I find a magnifying glass with a built-in light extremely useful (photo 43). These are specifically made for embroiderers and can be obtained from embroidery or craft shops. The adjustable arm is easily attached to your work-bench.

Circular Table

It is possible to make a miniature table using cabinet-making techniques but I am not best qualified to advise about the method for doing so. You can achieve excellent results if you turn a table following the method outlined overleaf. The circular table shown here is made from a very dense piece of olive ash with an attractive grain in contrasting colours running through it.

45 Olive ash circular table
70mm (2³⁄₄in) in diameter with
setting for one

Turning

Turn the blank to fit into the compression jaws of a combination chuck. Next, turn the legs as you would the outside of a goblet bowl (Fig.32a(1)). Hollow the bowl (Fig.32a(2)) using standard end grain hollowing techniques (see page 54) and you can then turn the central column of the table (Fig.32b(3)) before parting off the table top. Part off the table top very carefully using a skew chisel to achieve a good finish from the tool. If necessary, finish off the top afterwards using a sanding disc.

Fig. 32a-c Dolls' house table

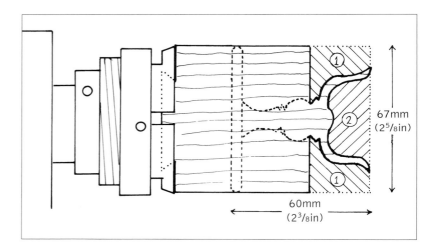

a First and second stages

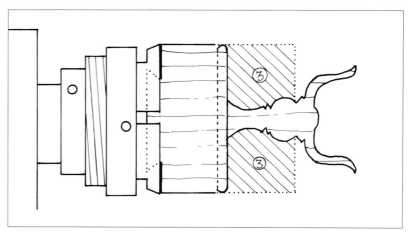

b Third stage

After parting off, the legs must be cut to shape as shown in Fig. 32c with a combination of small sanding discs, rifflers and carving burrs. It is important to mark out the legs accurately to start with. If you try to do it by eye, you will keep going round trying to make each leg match the one next to it and by the time you reach the last one, the difference between it and the first will be greater than you bargained for.

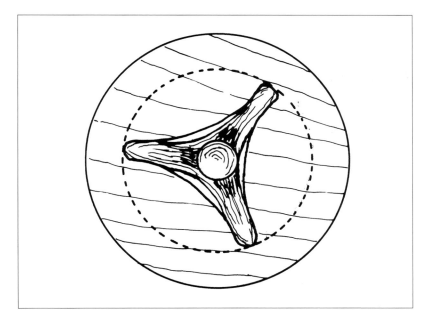

c Plan from underneath after shaping legs

Afterword

It is not possible to describe and illustrate all the great little things you can turn on a small lathe but I hope that this book will provide a series of challenging and enjoyable projects as well as inspiration for putting your own design ideas into practice.

It takes but a little imagination to turn a steak basher into a mallet if you leave out the grooves and give it a fatter head. By putting grooves on to a rolling pin, you can turn it into a pasta pin or breadcrumb grinder. There is an infinite number of differently shaped and sized boxes to be made: the smallest are suitable for dolls' houses; larger ones are ideal for jewellery or pills and larger ones still make excellent tea caddies.

It gives me the greatest satisfaction to make useful things but it is an even greater thrill to know that someone else finds them useful too. If this book encourages you to enjoy your hobby and make other people happy, it will have served its purpose.

Useful Addresses

Ashley Iles (Edge Tools) Ltd
WT9
East Kirby
Spilsby
Lincolnshire PE23 4DD
England

Axminster Power Tool Centre
Chard Street
Axminster
Devon EX13 5DZ
England

Carba-Tec (M & M Tools)
P O Box 128
Bexhill on Sea
East Sussex TN40 2QT
England

Clarke International
Lower Clapton Road
London E5 ORN
England

Craft Supplies Ltd
The Mill
Miller's Dale
Buxton
Derbyshire SK17 85N
England

Crown Tools Ltd
Burnt Tree Lane
Hoyle Street
Sheffield
South Yorkshire S3 7EX
England

Henry Taylor Tools Ltd
The Forge
Lowther Road
Sheffield
South Yorkshire S6 2DR
England

Jean Burhouse
The Old Sawmill
Inver
Dunkeld
Perth PH8 OJR
Scotland

John Boddy's
Riverside Sawmills
Boroughbridge
North Yorkshire YO5 9LJ
England

Klein Design Inc.
17910 SE 110th Street
Renton
WA 98059–5323
USA

Multistar Machine and Tool Ltd
Ashton House
Wheatfield Road
Colchester
Essex CO3 5YA
England

Nu-Tool Group
Carcroft Industrial Estate
Wellsyke Road
Adwick-le-Street
Doncaster
South Yorkshire DN6 7DU
England

C & M O'Donnell
Brough
Thurso
Caithness KW14 8YE
Scotland

Poolewood Equipment Ltd
Nottingham Airport
Tollerton Lane
Tollerton
Nottingham
Nottinghamshire NG12 4GA
England

Record Power Ltd
Parkway Works
Sheffield
South Yorkshire S9 3BL
England

Reg Sherwin
The Woodturner's Workshop
Avoncroft Museum of
Buildings
Stoke Heath
Bromsgrove
Worcestershire B60 4JR
England

Robert Sorby Ltd
Athol Road
Sheffield
South Yorkshire S8 OPA
England

The Working Tree
Milland
Liphook
Hampshire GU30 7JS
England

Tyme Machines
Paragon House
Flex Meadows
The Pinnacles
Harlow
Essex CM19 5TJ
England

Yandle and Sons
Hurst Works
Somerset TA12 6JU
England

Index